ON LITERACY

ON LITERACY

The Politics of the Word
from Homer to the Age of Rock

ROBERT PATTISON

OXFORD UNIVERSITY PRESS
Oxford   New York   Toronto   Melbourne

Oxford University Press

Oxford London Glasgow
New York Toronto Melbourne Auckland
Delhi Bombay Calcutta Madras Karachi
Kuala Lumpur Singapore Hong Kong Tokyo
Nairobi Dar es Salaam Cape Town

and associate companies in
Beirut Berlin Ibadan Mexico City Nicosia

Library of Congress Cataloging in Publication Data
Pattison, Robert.
On literacy.
Bibliography: p. Includes index.
1. Literacy. I. Title.
LC149.P33 001.2 82-3547
ISBN 0-19-503137-7 AACR2
ISBN 0-19-503423-6 (pbk.)

Grateful acknowledgment is made to the following for permission to quote material in copyright:

John Ashbery, "Paradoxes and Oxymorons," © 1980, 1981 by John Ashbery. Reprinted by permission of John Ashbery and Georges Borchardt, Inc.

W. H. Auden, "Marginalia," from *W. H. Auden: Collected Poems*, by W. H. Auden, edited by Edward Mendelson, Random House, Inc., © 1976. Used by permission.

T. S. Eliot, "East Coker," from *Four Quartets* by T. S. Eliot, © 1943 by T. S. Eliot; renewed 1971 by Esme Valerie Eliot. Reprinted by permission of Harcourt Brace Jovanovich, Inc.

Bruce Springsteen, "Jungleland," © 1975 by Bruce Springsteen and Laurel Canyon Music Ltd. Used by permission.

Pete Townshend, "Pure and Easy," copyright © 1972 by Fabulous Music Limited. Reprinted by permission of Towser Tunes, Inc.

Printing (last digit): 9 8 7 6 5 4 3 2 1
Printed in the United States of America

Preface

We are inadequately literate in part because we have inadequate ideas about literacy. This book seeks to improve our literacy by defining the term accurately.

My interest in defining literacy began while teaching freshman English in community colleges around New York. Interest is too mild a word. Freshman writing is a barrage of intellectual and social challenges masquerading as prose. Do these students write less literately than earlier generations? Are their mechanical errors symptomatic of cultural decline? Are they errors at all? Has television warped their capacity for literate behavior? How seriously will their deviation from the accepted norms of literate behavior affect their hopes for employment and advancement? In short, what does it mean to be literate?

Readers impatient for my answers to these questions should turn immediately to the last four chapters of this book. Readers curious to know why they should believe my answers should begin with Chapter One and read straight through. The early chapters describe the general conditions of literacy by examining its operation in past societies. The later chapters set our contemporary problems in the framework of this cultural history.

The present condition of literacy in America evokes concern bordering on despair from social commentators, educators, and ordinary citizens. This book is a reply to their anxiety. Taken in the right spirit, it is an answer that should comfort them. Literacy as I define it is always changing. We're not getting dumber, only older. Television is not a threat to development. The collapse of standard English need not presage a dark, merely a new age. My view of the present condition of our literacy only makes sense, though, if the word is redefined to accord with historical realities and purged of the connotations foisted upon it by modern orthodoxy.

My notes for this essay dismiss a number of works on literacy with three uncharitable words: same old whine. The same old whine can be heard in scholarly articles, in high-school English classes, in newspaper editorials, at PTA meetings, and at cocktail parties. It is an American—really an international—dogma. Whatever its incarnation, the same old whine is characterized by faith in four axioms: (1) that literacy is equivalent to skill in reading and writing; (2) that individuals who are literate by this standard are more cultured or civilized than those who are not; (3) that the skills of reading and writing should be propagated among poor peoples as a first step in their economic and social development; (4) that the skills of reading and writing should be preserved and expanded at home as a chief means of protecting democracy, moral values, rational thought, and all we hold dear.

In this book I deny or amend each of these premises, and suggest the following general conclusions in their place: (1) that literacy is foremost consciousness of the problems posed by language, and secondarily skill in the technologies, such as rhetoric and writing, by which this consciousness is expressed; (2) that different cultures may have different concepts of language and different technologies to express these concepts; thus there can be no universal standard of literacy;

(3) that economic and social development depends on a pragmatic concept of the uses of language shared among the leadership of the evolving community, and therefore imposition of narrow Western ideas about literacy on developing populations at home or abroad is not automatically beneficial; (4) that literacy changes in step with changing notions about language and with new technologies, and American literacy is currently undergoing a fundamental redefinition of literacy. This redefinition is neither good nor bad, but mindless resistance to it in the name of preserving deliquescent concepts of language and unadapted technologies of language-use is almost certainly fatal to the preservation of culture.

What follows, then, is a radical critique of the term literacy and its popular uses, which are usually unfounded in fact and destructive in practice. A radical critique in two senses. The conclusions I reach in the later part of the book confound prevailing beliefs about the virtues of reading and writing. In this sense the book is politically radical. But in order to reach my conclusions about literacy, I have examined the concept radically, at its historical roots. The politically radical conclusions of this book are built on a historically radical investigation of the basic components of literacy.

The book is designed so that each chapter serves two purposes, to examine a theoretical question connected with literacy and to study one historical period that illuminates the theoretical question. I have arranged the chapters so that the historical periods are presented chronologically.

Chapter One examines common usages of the word literacy and argues that the term has broad significance, like the concepts described by the words politics and economics. Literacy is mechanical ability with the technologies of language coupled with consciousness of language as a force in human affairs. The technologies of language—rhetoric, reading, writing—are the subject of Chapter Two. I have set the discussion of the fundamental attributes of these skills in the context of ancient history, the period when reading and writing have the most clearly defined impact on the growth of culture. The technologies of literacy have some general characteristics that apply in all cultures, but generally it is useless to discuss reading and writing as abstract forces. They can only be understood as part of the society that uses them.

Not every society has chosen to use literacy in the same way, but literacy is always connected with power. Chapter Three looks at the attitudes about language that shaped the competing literacies of classical and Christian civilization. Each of these literacies generated power for the ruling elements in society, but these were very different kinds of power and very different elites. The victory of the Christian concept of Word as literacy has helped to shape the direction of our culture and is probably more important in itself than the advent of print technology, a historical event examined in Chapter Four. The technologies of print, and, in our own day, television, do not in themselves do anything to change the mental habits of civilization. They work to channel or intensify already existing concepts of literacy. Our concepts about language probably do more to determine the use we make of technology than technology does to determine our concepts about language, but consciousness and technology always have a reciprocal relation, and no two societies will have an identical relation between these two forces; that is, no two societies will have the same literacy.

Modern liberalism holds that literacy is an essential feature of human development, both mental and economic. Chapter Five challenges both these simplistic theses through an evaluation of the role of reading and writing in several nations and through a skeptical appraisal of the benefits of mechanical literacy skills in ordinary American life. Seen in a skeptical light, the sad reality of our society is not that so many have difficulty with reading and writing skills but that so many have become hysterical when they discuss our supposed failure of literacy. Chapter Six treats contemporary social hysteria about literacy as a symptom of a more pervasive social disorder: the attempt of the established classes to impose their beliefs on society by imposing their norms of language use.

Our generation has witnessed the strongest challenge since the age of Locke to the middle-class literacy that has dominated Anglo-American culture for the last 200 years. Chapter Seven describes the competing literacies of twentieth-century America—the literacy of the prevailing middle classes and the literacy of rock. No one, I think, can be sure how the confrontation between these two opposed ideologies, reflected in opposed media and opposed generations, will end. In a brief postscript, Chapter Eight, I mention my own thoughts on this subject and briefly propose an ideal form of training to achieve the best and most widely disseminated literacy.

None of these chapters is exhaustive. I often isolate one man or one incident to stand as an example of intricate social or intellectual trends. What this method gains in simplicity and clarity, it must always lose in depth and complexity. Literacy is a subject about which so much nonsense has been written, however, that I have thought it best to write a book that errs on the side of directness. I have written in what I hope is clear English designed to be accessible to the widest audience. For those who are already familiar with the literature on literacy, this book may serve as a stimulant to revaluation. For those who come fresh to the subject, the book can serve as a general introduction. It is largely for those who would like a general introduction that I have added bibliographical notes for each chapter, though I have also used these notes as a means of acknowledging the sources of ideas and information. The text itself is uncluttered by footnotes and scholarly apparatus. When I quote directly, I provide the sources in a separate section of notes at the end of the book, keyed to the author's name or the title of the work as mentioned in the text.

Literacy is something bigger and better than mechanical skill in reading and writing. Literacy is a potent form of consciousness. Once possessed, it makes us productive. It irradiates the universe we have created. It remakes our lives. It gives us power for good and ill—more often for ill in proportion as we misunderstand it. I hope by understanding it better we may finally have more of it.

I acknowledge with gratitude the assistance of the Rockefeller Foundation, whose fellowship allowed me the time to write the book. Bill Roberson and Valerie Parry of the Southampton College library invested time and effort in locating material for me. The librarians of UNESCO and the Bureau of the Census were very kind—the librarian at the Census Bureau not only helped me on the phone but sent a load of free and very useful books. I wish I knew her name to thank her. The many bonehead English students I have taught who first compelled me to ask myself what literacy is deserve special thanks.

R. P.

Southampton, N. Y.
June, 1982

Contents

ON LITERACY

CHAPTER ONE

Blithering Agamemnon: The Borders of Literacy

Congratulations. Because you can read and transcribe this sentence, you are considered by every country of the United Nations to be literate. In some countries this ability would place you in a decided minority—in Afghanistan, for instance, you would be among an elite 12 percent of the population. In the United States, however, your literacy consigns you to the majority. According to the latest government figures on literacy, only 1 percent of the American public is incapable of reading and writing, and this small fraction consists largely of elderly, black farmworkers.

Other concepts of literacy have lately begun to undermine the reassuring mechanical certainty of government statistics. The work of UNESCO, of Marshall McLuhan, of anthropologists, of linguists, of social historians, of every elementary, secondary, and now college teacher too is increasingly concerned with some sense of the word literacy, and not always in the straightforward sense of reading and writing skills.

Few people today agree on the term's definition. Each writer on the subject defines the word anew or qualifies it with an adjective. We have scholarly articles and public debates on functional literacy, on full literacy, on semi-literacy, on pre-literacy, and even on super-literacy—a state supposedly achieved by minorities who use illiteracy as a form of rebellion by which they scorn their oppressors. Anthropologists and social historians must define literacy for each study they undertake. One writer on the Middle Ages calls literate all those who can read or write in any language; another insists that to be literate the medieval man had to have a reading knowledge of Latin. The United States Census Bureau has measured literacy in two ways—in one test by the ability to read and write simple messages in any language, in another by years of schooling. The army on the other hand applies a functional definition—does the person read and write well enough to understand written instructions? Sociologists have devised still other measures of functional literacy, and these do not exhaust the possible uses of the term. We need a universal definition of literacy for scholar and ordinary citizen alike, applicable to the past and present and serviceable for the future. What follows is an attempt at such a definition.

LITERACY AND CONSCIOUSNESS

Two very different senses of literacy exist side by side in common English usage. If I say, "A census conducted in 1962 indicates that 98.5 percent of all Upper Voltans are illiterate," most people will assume I mean that the vast majority of the population of Upper Volta lacks the technical skills of reading and writing. I would be making no judgment of the Upper Voltan mind or character, any more than I would be if I observed that most Tibetans cannot drive cars. But if a New Yorker remarks that most Californians he has met are illiterate, few will misinterpret him to mean that they cannot read or write. His statement is a studied insult to some basic aspect of Californians' intelligence. Do these two widely different usages have anything in common? Are we justified in using one word to embrace so many phenomena?

I think the answer to both these questions is yes. Literacy may not be a term like justice or goodness, for which philosophers have sought enduring metaphysical definitions, but it may usefully be compared to terms like agriculture and politics, which denote broad but recognizable areas of human activity. We can appreciate that diverse phenomena like Vergil's *Georgics,* Malthus's *Essay on Population,* and McCormick's reaper have an interest in common that we can call agricultural. Without doing violence to the word politics, we can profitably employ it for a fuller understanding of the operation of the Soviet Union, of Eskimo tribes, and of university faculties. The English word literacy lends itself to a similarly wide significance. It denotes consciousness of the questions posed by language coupled with mastery of those skills by which a culture at any given moment in its history manifests this consciousness.

Different people and different societies will be conscious of themselves as users of language in different ways, and will display their awareness in different media and with different skills, yet each may be called literate. Over the last four hundred years reading and writing have been the primary skills by which Western civilization has expressed its consciousness of itself as a language-using organism, and so we are accustomed to regard the attainment of these talents as synonymous with literacy itself, but our own common usage and that of other cultures belies so simple an equation. On some occasions, Aristotle uses the Greek word for illiteracy, *agrammatia,* to mean the inability to read or write; on others, he uses it in a broader sense to mean the lack of awareness of the uses of language. He even applies the term to animals: some animals have a voice, and, of these, some make ordered, mutually intelligible sounds, while others simply make noise without any purpose or organization. These last beasts Aristotle calls illiterate. This sense of the word must be something like what Rebecca West means when, in a letter to the *Times Literary Supplement* attacking a biography in which she is quoted, she says, "I appear throughout the book as dispensing gossip in a vulgar and illiterate manner." In other words, she believes the offending author to have portrayed her as someone who expatiates without any consciousness or control of her language. The New Yorker who chides the Californian must have a similar definition in mind.

Consciousness of the uses and problems of language is the foundation of literacy, but the literate person must also be able to express this consciousness in the ways evolved and sanctioned by the culture in which he lives. At present American culture anticipates that its members shall be able to read and write, and for us these skills are an intimate part of any definition of literacy. But some cultures do not demand these specific accomplishments as part of their definition of literacy. Cicero, speaking of the great Roman orators of the generations preceding his, calls one *litteratus* because of his fine sense for the right word and another *litteratius*—more literate than his contemporaries—because he was better spoken. Cicero is using the Latin word from which our term literate comes, but in his mind the foremost skill requisite to the full expression of one's literacy is not reading or writing, but rhetoric. By the American definition, Homer, whoever he might have been, was an illiterate because he almost certainly could neither read nor write, but I doubt it occurred to the Athenians of the fourth century B.C. to think of him as we do of high-school dropouts.

The question "Was Homer literate?" makes sense only when we have a clear notion of literacy in mind. If we insist that literacy is, was, and always will be what the West in the twentieth century defines it to be, then he was not. But if we allow each age to express literacy for itself, within the broad guideline that literacy must always refer to consciousness of language and skill in deploying this consciousness, then Homer was the paragon of literacy for the Greek world. To say that Homer was illiterate is something like saying that ancient Sparta had no economy because it wasn't capitalistic. It would be more useful to say that Homer exemplifies the literacy that flourished in the Greek world of the archaic period, but that he did not know how to read or write.

Literacy is a combination of variables—individual and cultural awareness of language and the interplay of this awareness with the means of expression. This approach will frustrate anyone looking for a simple, mechanical definition because it distinguishes between the attainment of reading and writing skills and the acquisition of literacy. Reading and writing may be parts of literacy but do not constitute the whole. Anyone accustomed to thinking of literacy as a fixed, moral quality will, I suspect, also be thwarted by this concept of the term. The distinguished critic Douglas Bush once cited as illiterate a verbal blunder in one of John Connally's campaign speeches. The Texan called for a "more virulent"—instead of a "more virile"—national defense. "A hundred years ago, when educated people were literate," Bush lamented, such a gaffe would not have occurred. Implicit in his judgment is a moral reproach to the present age. Many people use the word literacy to denote a state of mental enlightenment, an ideal realization of human intelligence, that either existed in the past and is now corrupted by the likes of John Connally or toward which the world is evolving, albeit slowly. Bush's comment locates a literate utopia in the educated society of "a hundred years ago"—when, wonderfully, no word was ever misspelled or misspoken, at least not among that fraction of the population constituting "educated people." Nonsense of this order defeats any attempt to set the study of literacy on an objective foundation. The term literacy is not profitably employed to condemn one age for not replicating the attitudes or skills enjoyed by another. And a word in Connally's defense. He may need some help with his vocabulary, but who would call the man illiterate after his Watergate performance? Tried and acquitted of a bribery charge in the Götterdämmerung of the Nixon administration, Connally later ran for the Presidency with the reassuring argument that he was the only candidate in the race who had been proven to be not guilty. Connally is certainly conscious of language and its uses. His rationale may not have been good politics, but it is essentially literate.

To say that literacy involves consciousness by individuals and cultures of the uses of language immediately elicits fundamental questions. What is meant by "consciousness" and "language"? Doesn't the use of language necessarily demand consciousness? The study of literacy does not, fortunately, require a definitive statement on either consciousness or language. If it did, it could never begin. The object of any investigation into literacy should be to discover the roles that individuals and civilizations at given moments believe consciousness and language play in their lives and to study how these ideas are manifested, both in the mechanics of expression and more broadly in the life of the culture. At the outset, it is only necessary for the student of literacy to believe that consciousness and language do in fact exist and that they might have some influence on the conduct of human affairs.

No one is likely to argue the existence of language or its influence on the lives of men. But there are enough skeptics about the existence of consciousness to demand a justification of this term. I use the term in its most mundane sense. As I type this page, I am conscious that words appear on the paper in front of me and that I or someone else might alter these words in ways that I imagine might change a reader's sense of my intention. I may have no free will to choose the words I write; they may be determined. But part of me believes I might have chosen other words. This part I call consciousness. Whether or not my freedom exists, my assertion of freedom is demonstrable.

Defined this way, even a behaviorist can accept consciousness. The behaviorist might even acquiesce in the important corollary to this definition: that not all people are conscious of language in the same way. The poet may attribute his poetry to divine inspiration; his audience, to gin. Whether either party is correct in its interpretation of consciousness does not concern the investigator of literacy. For him it does not matter if consciousness does or does not exist, but only that people believe that it does. He is curious to know what the various theories of consciousness are and how they affect the poet, the poetry, and the culture in which they appear. Consciousness of language here is a description of the relations people believe to exist between language, the mind, and the world.

Most people go through the day without often exercising their consciousness of language. If they did, society would be either surfeited with literature and brilliant conversation or paralyzed by silence. To be aware of every word and its ramifications might be either sublime or petrifying. Yet consciousness of language is innately human. It shows itself most obviously in puns, slang, rhyme, and the host of verbal tricks. Charles the Bald, the royal patron of the ninth-century philosopher Scotus Erigena, once baited his distinguished client by asking him over dinner, "What's the difference between a Scot and a sot?" The pun on the philosopher's name demonstrates the rudiments of literacy. Charles was as aware as any child of the possibilities of manipulating the world by manipulating language. Scotus's reply was "The table between us." Scotus was more literate than Charles.

Consciousness of the uses of language—the keystone of literacy—is in fact diffused throughout mankind, without apparent regard to social or economic factors. Different styles of education in the uses of language, however, may shape this consciousness in diverse ways. The judge who sentences an indigent defendant to a twenty-five-year jail term has disciplined his consciousness of language by the study of the written code of law, its ambiguities, and its interpretation. He is in this sense literate. But the defendant who cries out as he is led from the court, "This ain't no fuckin' justice," is literate after his own fashion. He is conscious of a discrepancy between his notion of the word "justice" and the actual processes of the social order. The student of literacy is not obliged to decide between the literacy of judge and defendant, but he ought to be interested in noting which form of literacy prevails in various social arenas like the courtroom.

The literate man who has understood that a discrepancy exists can then go on to decide whether he wishes to assign a higher degree of validity to language or to the phenomena it describes—perhaps he may wish to deny validity to both. In any event, the perception of the original discontinuity between language and events and the attempt to resolve it are early stages of literacy. On the attitudes they generate rest the various forms of literate behavior.

The recognition that language and its objects do not perfectly correspond is so fundamental that we may wonder if it is possible to be human without it. Three instances of this basic sort of illiteracy come to mind: the Wild Boy of Aveyron, Gracie Allen, and Homer's Agamemnon.

THE WILD BOY
AND GRACIE ALLEN

When he was discovered roaming the French countryside in 1800, the Wild Boy of Aveyron could not speak or understand any language. He was somewhere around twelve years old at the time. Though his senses and health seemed unimpaired, he subsequently failed to learn how to speak, and his ability to manipulate written signs and letters of the alphabet remained inferior to the performance it is now possible to elicit from chimpanzees in language experiments. Bruno Bettelheim has diagnosed the Wild Boy as an autistic child, while other learning specialists point out that language is attained by humans at a definite time within a sequence of developmental steps, and that the Wild Boy, having missed proper training at the appropriate time, forever forfeited access to language. Whatever his case, we may take the Wild Boy as a model illiterate: unable to speak, read, write, and unaware of any relation in his life between mind, language, and reality.

The Wild Boy's lack of the mechanical language skills of speech, reading, and writing, however, is not the sole determinant of his illiteracy. If it were, then Helen Keller would also have to be classified as illiterate. But surely no one would call Helen Keller illiterate. Whatever her handicaps, the consciousness of language was alive in Helen Keller from an early age. In her autobiographical essays, *The World I Live In*, she makes it clear that for her the acquisition of language is the beginning of consciousness, of thought, of humanity:

> Before my teacher came to me, I did not know that I am. I lived in a world that was a no-world. I cannot hope to describe adequately that unconscious yet conscious time of nothingness. I did not know that I knew aught, or that I lived or acted or desired. I had neither will nor intellect. . . .
>
> Since I had no power of thought, I did not compare one mental state with another. So I was not conscious of any change or process going on in my brain when my teacher began to instruct me. I merely felt keen delight in obtaining more easily what I wanted by means of the finger motions she taught me: When I learned the meaning of "I" and "me" and found that I was something, I began to think. Then consciousness first existed for me. Thus it was not the sense of touch that brought me knowledge. It was the awakening of my soul that first rendered my

senses their value, their cognizance of objects, names, qualities, and properties. Thought made me conscious of love, joy, and all the emotions.

For Helen Keller, as for many modern philosophers and linguists, language is the indispensable human attribute, the means by which we know ourselves and the world. Once we possess it, we enter into a dialogue with life by which both we and the world are continually the richer:

> I came later to look for an image of my emotions and sensations in others. I had to learn the outward signs of inward feelings. . . . Groping, uncertain, I at last found my identity, and after seeing my thoughts and feelings repeated in others, I gradually constructed my world of men and of God. As I read and study, I find that this is what the rest of the race has done. Man looks within himself and in time finds the measure and meaning of the universe.

To be conscious of oneself as a user of language—to master "the outward signs of inward feelings"—is to begin to take the measure of creation. For Helen Keller, the use of signs is the germ of all ideas, the starting point for life.

By this standard, the Wild Boy of Aveyron, locked in the dark and languageless confines of his undeveloped mind, does seem to be the prototypical illiterate. It is only fair to note, however, that other observers believe consciousness and thought exist beyond and before language. For Piaget, "the structuration characteristic of intelligence" precedes all the modes of expression—some primary ability to organize events in the mind comes before and in part determines the uses of language. Gilbert Ryle and philosophers of the positivist school also hold that thought can be divorced from any mode of expression. Perhaps they are right. In speaking or writing, people will often remark that they would like to say exactly what they think, as if the thought was an entity that needed translation into language rather than being itself a

verbal event. Jean-Marc-Gaspard Itard, the doctor who cared
for the Wild Boy, once purposely punished his mute ward
without reason, even though the boy had just performed a
lesson to perfection. The boy was not merely confused and
morose, as animals are when unjustly or unintelligibly punished; he was indignant. Did he, without language, understand the concept of justice? If he did, then perhaps we do
live in a world of transcendent realities generally known to
us in the imprecise medium of language but present to us
with or without language—a world quite different from the
one Helen Keller describes.

Whichever view is correct, the Wild Boy must still be
considered an illiterate. Whatever language does for us, he
did not possess a consciousness of its uses or any skill in its
deployment. His case, though, and the debates that surround
it, may serve as a warning that literacy, even literacy in the
fundamental sense we have been discussing, is not a magical
attribute that defines the uniqueness of man. The Wild Boy
possessed some essential humanity beyond the uses of consciousness and language. His teacher Itard felt the boy's humanity. Truffaut celebrated it in *L'Enfant sauvage*. Even
total illiteracy does not strip us of our humanity. Nor can we
be sure that other species do not possess some sort of literacy.
It may be that dolphins or whales pass many fruitful hours in
the consciousness of themselves as users of language and the
manipulation of their means of expression. We do not know,
nor does it matter. For the moment it is only important to
point out that the study of literacy is from the beginning involved in some way with the nature of thought, of mind, and
of language.

I pick Gracie Allen to represent another basic type of
illiteracy, though any number of similar comic types would
suffice to define it—Stan Laurel, Chico Marx, Shakespeare's
clowns. But not Shakespeare's fools. A Shakesperian fool is
always literate. Touchstone is a master of language, and

Lear's fool knows better than his master the discrepancy that exists between language and the practice of the world. The clown, however, is generally impervious to the questions posed by language.

The clown carries insensitivity to language to its absurd, illiterate extreme. He operates like a computer, capable of spewing forth words, sentences, puns, *aperçus*, but unconscious of what he does. The illiterate clown is a producer but never a consumer of wit. Though he can speak, and perhaps even read and write (in *A Night at the Opera* Chico Marx can read the famous contract even though he won't be fooled by its Santa-ty Claus), he is devoid of any critical awareness of language. For the clown, language is simple and inflexible, habitual but unconscious. Not everyone appreciates clown humor, but it is an enduring element of culture. Here are Burns and Allen in an early vaudeville routine:

> *Gracie:* On my way in, a man stopped me at the stage door and said, "Hiya, cutie, how about a bite tonight after the show?"
>
> *George:* And you said?
>
> *Gracie:* I said, "I'm busy after the show, but I'm not doing anything now," so I bit him.
>
> *George:* Gracie, let me ask you something. Did the nurse ever happen to drop you on your head when you were a baby?
>
> *Gracie:* Oh no, we couldn't afford a nurse, my mother had to do it.

The clown is programmed to understand language only in its most literal form. He cannot adjust for context, tone, or nuance.

The illiterate clown is a creature of the stage. It is difficult to imagine that there are many—or any—people as obtuse to the uses of language as the Gracie Allen of vaudeville.

It is even harder to imagine a whole culture sunk in illiteracy of this sort. Like the Wild Boy of Aveyron, the clown is a freak, a rarity. The clown is a literary type, a recurring figure of the imagination. He returns age after age in various guises to remind audiences of their own literacy, for to laugh at the clown is to celebrate one's own consciousness of the problem of language.

AGAMEMNON AND THE PHYSICAL
BASIS OF LITERACY

My third type of fundamental illiterate is Homer's Agamemnon, leader of the Greeks against Troy. Several years ago Julian Jaynes's book *The Origin of Consciousness in the Breakdown of the Bicameral Mind* announced that what we call consciousness was a phenomenon unknown to the Greeks of Homer's time; that the right and left hemispheres of the brain were not then neurologically related as they are now; and that certain critical mental activity occurring in the right hemisphere, which is now fodder for conscious reflection, appeared to the characters of the *Iliad* as divine and external voices completely detached from self. "The gods take the place of consciousness," Jaynes says; Agamemnon "did not have any ego whatever."

Jaynes's thesis, while indefensible, provokes a series of stimulating questions. If the voices of Agamemnon's right and left hemispheres are indeed unaware of belonging to the same mind, and if we accept the definition that he is therefore unconscious and egoless, then Agamemnon is certainly illiterate in the widest sense of the term. He is a simple automaton responding to stimuli within his own body over which he exercises no control. Nor, lacking consciousness, can he reflect on the stimuli themselves. Is this an accurate portrait of the character Homer depicts? Were the minds of Homer and the Greek heroes similarly constituted? Does the kind of literacy we have been discussing have a biological basis, as Jaynes's argument implies?

No doubt Homer's Agamemnon is a type of illiterate. From the first lines of Book I when he insults Apollo's priest Chryses he is insensitive to or unconscious of the effect his words have. He either ignores or does not hear the advice of the Greek leaders given in counsel. When Zeus sends him a false dream assuring him of easy victory, he accepts the prophecy uncritically and persuades the army to act upon it, thereby initiating the brutal and indecisive warfare of the poem. Plain-spoken Diomedes tells the king to his face that before they can reckon with the Trojans, the Greeks must deal with Agamemnon's folly. Homer's portrait of the leader of the Danaan host is by no means flattering, though it is relieved by human touches throughout: Agamemnon shows much brotherly concern for his often incompetent brother Menelaus, and elsewhere he admits his own confusion to Nestor. But Jaynes is in the main correct. Agamemnon is a man seemingly driven by voices and emotions whose source he neither knows nor cares to scrutinize. He is a robot, and even though he is a character from an age that had not yet adopted reading and writing, he may more justly be called illiterate because of his insensitivity to speech, thought, and their relation to action.

But if Agamemnon uncritically accepts false dreams, divine but misleading voices, and his own unexamined verbiage, neither Homer nor the other Greeks do. Diomedes points out the king's rhetorical weakness. Nestor, universally respected for his age and good counsel, is skeptical of any line of action dictated by a dream and accepts Agamemnon's dream only because he is the man in charge. By Book XIX, when Agamemnon apologizes to Achilles and justifies his behavior with an ornate argument that shifts the blame from himself onto Fate and the gods, the Greeks are weary of the quarrel and happy to be once again united, but Achilles has no patience with the king's elaborate mythological justification. To Agamemnon's contention that "I am not at fault, but Zeus and Fate and the Erinys," Achilles replies, "Let us think of the battle immediately. It is not proper to waste further time or breath here. The great work still remains undone." The word with which Achilles dismisses Agamemnon's attempt to justify himself is particularly acute. It occurs in Greek literature only at this place: *klotopeuein,* to blither—"to waste time in false pretenses," as Liddell and Scott's dictionary has it. Agamemnon is an illiterate in the full sense of the word, and his compatriots know it. One narrative strand of the *Iliad* deals with the blight of illiteracy as it perverts the actions of men. Homer is as alive as Jaynes to Agamemnon's failure of consciousness. He treats it as one dimension of the human tragedy.

The clown and the Wild Boy are extreme, perhaps even idealized, types of illiterates. The illiteracy we are more likely to encounter in life is Agamemnon's sort, and Homer knew that illiteracy of this kind is no stranger to high places. The failure of men to exercise their consciousness upon the problems posed by language is no isolated mishap, nor is it necessarily connected with the mechanical skills of reading and writing. Each culture may evolve its own forms of consciousness and its own values for language—Homer's are not our own—but without some forms and values, there can hardly be said to be culture at all.

Both consciousness and language—and therefore literacy—depend to some extent on the brain. No brain, no language, no consciousness, no literacy. Research in the physical basis of language and consciousness has increased dramatically from the time of Paul Broca in the last century. Neither the location nor the organization of language faculties in the brain, however, is certainly known. This is putting it mildly. Language skills were once thought to depend on the left hemisphere of the brain. Recent studies indicate, however, that both hemispheres have capacities for language, though these differ in quality and purpose. The physical basis of consciousness is a question even more vexed than that of language. Not everyone agrees that something called consciousness really exists, and few can agree upon a definition of the term. In addition, attempts to locate the origin of so grand and mysterious a process in some one area of the brain, however legitimate, seem at times as silly as Descartes's endeavor to prove that the soul resides in the pineal gland of the brain.

Nevertheless, despite the complexities of the relation between consciousness and the body, consciousness may undergo physical change. The physical resources that the brain devotes to various tasks do appear to be in a state of flux—why not the capacity for consciousness itself? If the neurologists are correct in their assumptions about the development of the human brain, then over time—perhaps millennia, perhaps mere centuries—areas of the brain originally controlling one function—say smell or taste—have been co-opted by the evolutionary process and devoted to new activities. Some researchers believe that the amount of brain space devoted to the language skills has increased and continues to do so. It's a fair assumption that if the brain is in a state of physical evolution, then consciousness, whatever it may be, is too.

The welter of neurological data and speculation confirms that literacy must not be treated as a constant in human affairs but as an evolving and adaptable attribute of the species. Some conclusion of this sort is obvious. Writing, for instance, requires a certain amount of evolved dexterity. Speech depends upon the evolution of those areas of the brain named after pioneer neurologists Broca and Wernicke. The question of evolution and literacy becomes trickier, however, when we ask if the modern mind possesses some physical capacity for language not enjoyed by, say, the ancient Egyptians. Can we absorb more language than they? Can we apply language to areas of experience that they could not because of cerebral incapacity? One of the cruces of ancient history, for instance, is the failure of the classical world to exploit scientific technology as we do. Did this failure stem solely from a social or economic reluctance to apply scientific knowledge in a systematic fashion or was it abetted by the physical underdevelopment of those brain systems that are necessary for effective use of scientific ideas? The questions themselves, no matter what their answers, remind us that literacy as a function of the brain is rooted in history in its largest sense. Literacy like man himself changes in time.

The neurological evidence supports the conclusion that all of man's mental activity is colored by language. But according to the best evidence, the language faculty is not located in some central brain site. It is not a computer center in the university of the mind. The language abilities—and the same may be true of the sources of consciousness—are scattered throughout the brain. Different areas seem to have lives of their own. In one experiment a patient whose left and right hemispheres had been surgically separated had at least two areas of his brain that maintained different opinions about his future occupation. The left hemisphere wanted to be a draughtsman, the right an auto racer. In another case, a proctologist whose language faculties seemed to have been crippled so badly that he could not make simple requests was nonetheless alert enough to deliver an eloquent denunciation of Preparation H. Under clinical conditions, scientists can observe another fascinating phenomenon: the mind in the process of lying. The talkative left hemisphere, when asked questions to which only the separated right hemisphere knows the answers, will nevertheless respond with certainty and bravado. At least part of our language system is desperate for omniscience and behaves like any New Yorker when asked for directions. When you want to go to the Bronx, he will send you to Brooklyn rather than admit he does not know the way. The language function in man may come with so strong an urge for assertion that it willingly sacrifices connections between words and the world to its need for order and dominance.

Language skills are not centrally located in one section of the brain, but widely diffused. Some parts of the brain appear to exercise greater control than others over specific language functions like speech, reading, and writing. According to neurologists, vocabulary is stored throughout the mind, and perhaps different areas keep double copies of words and syntactic forms, just as libraries buy multiple copies of books for different collections. The neurological evidence suggests that language is not a single mental function but a diverse set of phenomena drawing on a variety of the brain's resources. All the technologies of literacy—reading, writing, rhetoric, electronic media—are creatures of mind, and they share its diversity. They have their own characters.

Literacy is a function of the brain as diverse and devious in its workings as its source. Like the brain, from which it proceeds, literacy is a composite of many aptitudes, not all of which are equally developed or genuine. If consciousness of language evolves, then literacy is in historical flux. If language is the medium by which the brain asserts its omniscience, even at the cost of fabrication, then literacy is in part the formal structure society gives to its lies.

The student of literacy need not approach the subject with any particular creed about language. He ought to be aware, however, that behind the social data usually employed to discuss the topic lies a breathtaking world of ideology that arises from the solutions imposed upon the problems of language. These solutions make up the tenets essential to the formation of a literate culture. The culture that believes language is foremost a mechanism by which the brain transfers information will have one kind of literacy. The culture that holds language to be the human attribute that mirrors divinity will have another. They will differ not only in theory but in social organization. The rest of this book is particularly concerned with the way various cultures treat the phenomenon of literacy. Before turning to the historical flux, however, let me say a few words to illustrate what I mean by "the problems presented by language." To clarify the point, I will take the most exalted view of language that I know.

LITERACY AND LANGUAGE

Philosophers of the ancient world and the early Church evolved the celebrated Logos doctrine, best known from the opening verses of the gospel according to St. John: "In the beginning was the Word, and the Word was with God, and the Word was God." Many volumes have been written to explicate the word Logos, but the translation of the Authorized Version is entirely apt. In the Logos doctrine, God is not merely thought to be like language in its most sublime sense, he is equated with it. In framing their thoughts the authors of the Logos doctrine were contemplating a rarefied notion of language as transcending though not divorced from mortal discourse. They intended to know the divinity by knowing his mode of being, language. We may profitably reverse their procedure and attempt to understand language better by asking why anyone would identify it with God.

According to this view, language, like God, is that in which "we live, and move, and have our being." It is not a separate and specialized attainment of human culture, like mathematics or architecture. Neither these nor any other branch of human intelligence could exist in the absence of language. It is unique, incomparable, universal. It would be foolish to imagine that there are competing systems of language—body language or sign language, for instance. No competing system of signs or signals makes the slightest sense except as it refers to language itself. Crossing my legs away from the person next to whom I sit may mean "I want to keep my distance from you," but it only means this if language exists. Meaning itself depends upon language. Mathematics may yet develop a system of signs free of the impurities of ordinary language, but these could never be explicable without language. Like God, language is beyond metaphor, the ubiquitous first cause of the mind.

Furthermore, whether there is in fact any order in the universe, or whether the human mind merely projects structures of its own devising upon creation, our sense of order is inextricably bound up with language. It may be that certain fundamental truths exist beyond language. The case of the Wild Boy who was indignant at a senseless punishment suggests that justice is a transcendent idea not dependent on but merely stated in language. Bertrand Russell argued that the notion of similarity is also a transcendent reality: phenomena really are similar, with or without language. Zen and Wittgenstein carry their doctrines to the limits of the utterable and point silently to a real Beyond, which, though much discussed, is supposed to be ineffable. None of these sublime speculations, however, could exist in the absence of language, and in practice our notions of order in the world and in ourselves are inseparable from the language in which we frame them. The famous statement of Descartes can be rewritten thus: "I am able to say 'I think, therefore I am'; therefore I am." Without the power of language, the *cogito* is nowhere—an observation certainly understood by the philosophers of the Logos doctrine, who seem implicitly to have believed that since language is all-pervasive, unique, and prior to the expression of any thought, it must therefore be the mode of divine order.

When Nietzsche comes to reevaluate the question of language for the modern period, he begins with the same premise as the authors of the Logos theory but alters their conclusion: the supposed order of the universe is only dependent on man the manipulator of words; man is free of an illusory obligation to some meaning in language beyond his own creation. Thus man himself is divine in his free and inventive use of language, by which he makes and controls the world.

The study of literacy is enmeshed in the philosophical speculation of which I have just given the merest précis. To judge of the relation between language and the universe is the essence of literacy, though literacy does not demand any specific judgment—the Logos-framers', Nietzsche's, or anyone else's. The act of judgment, no matter how misguided or naïve, is the first characteristic of literacy, and it precedes and embraces other forms of intelligence, though it does not exhaust them. Terms like "mathematical literacy," "scientific literacy," and "philosophical literacy" are at the moment much in vogue in the English-speaking world. These expressions refer to ease, breadth, and depth of knowledge in specific fields of study. But literacy as I have defined it is a necessary condition for any of these other intellectual accomplishments. There can be no scientific knowledge without language to give it form; nor could there be any knowledge at all unless the knower makes some sort of judgment of the relation between the words of an assertion and the part of the universe about which the assertion is made.

Language is the *primum mobile* of intellectual life. We can carry the likeness between deity and Logos a step further by observing that both the supreme being and language first realize themselves in speech. God says, "Let there be light," and there is light. God first speaks the Ten Commandments to Israel, only later condescending to write them down for a thick-headed people. Jesus conducts his ministry orally and himself makes no written record whatsoever. Marshall McLuhan and others have treated speech as technology and have stressed the differences between cultures that depend on the technology of speech and those that have developed the technologies of writing, print, and the electronic media. But speech is only technological by straining the definition of

technology beyond the limits of sense. Speech is a requisite
for the application of all other technologies. Writing is clearly
a technology, a human endeavor that like all technologies
constitutes a manipulation of the physical environment by
man. But the part of nature that writing seeks to organize—
language—is nothing but speech itself. Speech is required to
make sense of writing, as it is to understand any other technological achievement. If speech is technological, then it
must be called the technology of technologies. If speech is
technological, then so is the human brain and the beaver's
tail. But to call any of these technological is to confuse technology with evolution. Technology is the application man
makes of his brain and his capacity for language. It is not
synonymous with brain and language.

I make this point at length because much confusion results from the false assumption that speaking is a technology
that competes with and is similar to writing and other mechanical means of dealing with language. From this error
comes a hypothesis something like this: some cultures have
the technology of speech—these are oral cultures; others have
the more advanced technology of writing—these are writing
cultures. Their superior technology fundamentally alters the
mental and social organization of these written cultures just
as the application of iron or steam revolutionizes human ideology and social structure.

This appealing argument cannot survive exposure to common sense. All cultures are by definition oral cultures. When
men learn to write they do not then forget how to speak.
Even with writing, much information—probably most information necessary for fundamental human activity—continues
to be passed along solely by speech and held in the mind
without written records. Consider the roles speech and writing have played in the acquisition of those habits that constitute the framework of an average American morning. Smith
wakes up, turns off the alarm clock, turns on the light, gets

up, bathes, dresses, walks to the kitchen, boils water for coffee and fries eggs, eats, reads the paper, drives to work. Writing may have enriched his understanding of any or all of these acts—he may be an authority on cuisine or hygiene—but written instruction or help is not essential to the learning or the enjoyment of any of these daily activities. We are taught to bathe, dress, cook, and eat sufficiently by example and by spoken direction. We are necessarily taught how to read a newspaper not by reading some other piece of writing, but by speech. Even the complex mechanical task of driving the car is something most people master without any recourse to the written word. Driving instructors will testify to the number of educated clients who have mastered the rules of the road and assimilated the written instructions on driving but nonetheless cannot drive worth a damn. Would anyone want to be on the highway if the other drivers had learned solely by studying books?

Before leaving Smith on his way to work, we may note that though he does not live in a so-called oral culture, his mind is full of information that he has heard and memorized. He does not rely on written record for the bulk of the information that gets him through the day: his route to the office or factory, the location of the eggs and salt and pepper, the names of coworkers. This and most intelligence in the mind has been, is, and will in all likelihood remain a function of spoken language.

If language is the prime mover of human intelligence, speech is its first form. Before he has mastered any skill or technology, the literate person, unless physically impaired, must have become aware of himself as a speaker and have begun to examine the relation between the words he utters and the world in which he utters them. If and when he learns how to read, write, or operate a computer, this talent of examination is not lost or superseded, it is enhanced and redeployed.

Literacy begins for most of us with the scrutiny of speech —a tricky business, because speech is burdened with all the complexities of language itself. Examine the statement "I am looking at the river." Initially, we will need a human either to produce or to receive the statement. Assuming that our speaker is sound in wind and limb, and has therefore made his utterance in the way best calculated to produce distinct, intelligible sounds, we are further obliged to notice that he is speaking in English, using words and syntax peculiar to that language. Imagine that our speaker happens to be innocent of a knowledge of Spanish. As he crosses the border from El Paso into Juarez, does he become an illiterate? He certainly is no longer able to speak or understand the vocabulary or grammar of the native population.

Noam Chomsky would insist that our Spanish-free traveler was indeed literate wherever he might find himself. "The deep structure that expresses the meaning is common to all languages." Know one language, and you know the basis of all language. This observation is probably a limited consolation to our friend, who has now been reduced to inquiring for the lavatory by frantic gestures. But while the traveler cannot speak Spanish, and while his hypothetical knowledge of deep linguistic structure is of little practical value to him, I think we may still call him literate. Perhaps he is never more literate than when gesticulating because he is never more aware of the uses of language than when deprived of them. Literacy does not require a universal knowledge of language, only an awareness that language is a universal problem.

Within his own language, the speaker who says, "I am looking at the river," may be able to parse the sentence he speaks. He may in fact parse the sentence in the old or in the transformational grammar. Either is a literate activity, helpful to a better understanding of the relation of word, syntax, and meaning. But the speaker's friend who does not know how to parse a sentence in any grammar also engages in a literate activity when he notices that although his friend has uttered the words "I am looking at the river," he is in fact staring at his left shoe. Linguists are prone to use examples of language divorced from the contexts of life, but the literate person need not do so. Grammar has its place in the structure of literacy, but so does common sense, and common sense invites us to test speech against the world as a check upon meaning. If a man says he sees a river when in fact he looks at his shoe, his knowledge of grammar does not save him from what the world perceives as a physical or psychological defect.

But let us suppose our speaker in a concrete situation in which a river is actually before him. He is, in fact, standing at the windows of a Manhattan apartment overlooking the East River. In another room is his wife, who calls out, "What are you doing?" "I am looking at the river," he replies, turning away at the same moment to examine a stuffed alligator nearby. How are we to judge the relation of this utterance to the world in which it is made? Here is the man, there is the thing he calls the river. Some knowledgeable pest might correct our speaker for using the word river: the East River is in fact an estuary. Semantically, our friend is not quite accurate. Syntactically, he has also blundered, for at the moment he spoke the words, "I am looking," connoting a present and continuing action, he was in fact inspecting a stuffed alligator. Perhaps he ought to have said, "I was looking at the river," but that would not have answered his wife's question. Even if our speaker is in fact looking out the windows we cannot be sure that he is in fact looking at the river. He may be looking at the stewardess sunning herself in the nearby park. He may in fact be lying. Literacy must concern itself with the validity of language as well as its forms. Literacy intrudes on the domains of natural science, psychology, and ethics as well as linguistics.

Suppose our speaker has no alligator or stewardess before him and is in fact looking at what he believes to be a river. His statement presents us with several other difficulties. "I am looking at the river" may be for this man's wife a satisfactory explanation of his activities, but it is inadequate as a description of his full experience. Sight, thought, the organic functions of the perceiving body—the relation of mind, self, and world—are only feebly captured in "I am looking." Whatever the living actuality of water, movement, color, light, and traffic may be, it is imperfectly represented by the term "river." "Le monde s'exile dans le nom. A l'interieur, il y a le livre du monde." "The world loses itself in the word; within, there is the book of the world," writes the poet Edmond Jabès. Language rushes to encompass the world, which recedes before its embrace with equal speed. Whether the shadow of language can ever be reconciled with the reality which casts it is traditionally a problem of philosophy, but it is the business of literate investigation as well. Upon the answer we give to this question depend our ideas of validity, beauty, and utility in language. In our century, the philosophical and literate investigations of life have fused in the works of the logical positivists and of Heidegger, for whom the sentence "I am looking at the river" is a statement about Being that might best be understood by scrutinizing the least prominent word in the utterance: am. What does our speaker mean by this word? Heidegger's answer to the question of Being never loses sight of an obligation to know the relation between language and the world. The literacy of an age defines this relationship.

CHAPTER TWO

Chief Cobb vs. Themistocles: The Technologies of Rhetoric, Reading, and Writing

Before all else the literate man is alive to the problems of language. Not all the problems, perhaps, and certainly not all the time, but a vaudeville routine, a dream, or an epic poem can confront him with them. Simply to be awake to questions about the relation between language and life, however, is only a foundation, and on this foundation each society erects its own structure of literacy, compounded of theory and technology. Theories that respond to the questions of language give the structure its form. The available technology gives it its substance. We view the finished product as a unity and do not normally trouble ourselves to distinguish the components of literacy, but theory and technology are nonetheless distinguishable in the result as surely as are idea and marble in the construction of the Parthenon. The difficulty with rhetoric, reading, and writing is to discover what about them is absolute and unchanging from one culture to another and what about them is conditioned by social factors. This chapter attempts to sort out the problem in the context of ancient civilization.

RHETORIC

Speech is not one of the technologies of language; it is the fact about the world from which all technologies of language flow. Rhetoric, on the other hand, is a technology—the earliest technology of language. Except for illiterates like the Wild Boy, everyone has access to the world of language embodied in speech, but not everyone can use language to equal effect. Rhetoric, the art of using language to effect—the art of persuasion, as Aristotle has it—is a skill developed by men to exploit the natural resource of speech. The power of speech is like the ability to move one's limbs. Both are complex physical acts that depend upon training within the human community, but both are available to all men in the normal course of development. Rhetoric, though, is like etiquette, a learned social refinement of biological reality. The rhetorician aspires to reach and alter our consciousness. His is therefore a literate endeavor. He uses language in a studied way for result, thereby forming the raw matter of language by the technology of rhetoric. To be able to alter human affairs merely by opening one's mouth and making sounds that profess to deal in ideas is a powerful talent.

The value of rhetoric is rarely denied in the history of civilization, though the standards of rhetorical virtue may shift from culture to culture. Primitive peoples often display a dazzling command of rhetoric that confounds the so-called advanced civilizations that first come in contact with them. The eloquence of a Chief Seattle or a Chief Joseph has a Periclean dignity unexpected in societies otherwise technologically deficient. The technology of rhetoric, moreover, seems always to have been cultivated. Homer and the Bible celebrate the superior speaker, whether he is an Odysseus of many devices or a Jeremiah bent on salvation. Reading and writing skills were widespread in classical times, but rhetoric remained the keystone of education, whether in the Academy or the Church. The debauched heroes of the *Satyricon* and the early fathers of the Church studied in curricula that stressed the discipline of the spoken word. Rhetoric retained its central place in the medieval curriculum and survives in a lame form in the modern schoolroom. Handbooks of college English are still sometimes called "rhetorics," evidence of our society's insistence on reading and writing skills, which has divested the word of its traditional association with spoken language. On those few occasions when the primacy of rhetoric among the technologies of language has been questioned, the challenge has come from ideological extremists who doubt that eloquence furthers a quest for ultimate reality: anchorites reject not only rhetoric but language itself. They would have to. The rejection of rhetoric necessarily involves a condemnation of language.

Like any other technology, rhetoric becomes a commodity. The knowledge of rhetoric has a cost to the student, unlike the knowledge of speech. If there were a price-tag on speech, half the world would be mute. There is a price-tag on the talent of rhetoric, and through history most men have not been able to afford it. The technologies of language follow rhetoric in this: they are all part of the economic nexus of civilization. The technologies of language might be defined as those developments of language that have a cost to the user. The cost may be the purchase or payment of a teacher—language skills were often taught by slaves in the ancient world; today it is the custom to pay the instructor a token stipend—or the price may be exacted in time or trade. The medieval Church instructed pupils in the language arts, but usually with the stipulation, implied or stated, that the life of the pupil was to be devoted to the service of God. Even where instruction is given on grounds apparently eleemosynary, some form of bargain is always implied. The two competing methods of instructing the populations of develop-

ing nations in the skills of reading and writing are instances
of the economic realities of literacy. One method, championed by the American developmental educator Frank
Laubach, is a straightforward business arrangement. Pay the
instructor, and he teaches the book. The other, developed by
the progressive Brazilian educational theorist Paolo Freire,
has an idealistic, Marxist character. The instructor works
with his pupils as an equal, stimulating their powers of dialectic and political thinking at the same time as he teaches
reading and writing skills. The payment here is not monetary
but ideological. Just as the missionary expects his pupil to be
a Christian, Freire expects him to be a socialist. Whether
the medium of exchange is cash or ideas, however, the development of the talents of language belongs within the realm
of economics. One of the measures of the importance individuals and societies attach to particular technologies of
literacy will be how much they are willing to spend on it.

READING AND WRITING

While rhetoric is chief among the technologies of language, writing and the allied skill of reading are the talents
most commonly associated with the term literacy. I prefer to
call these attainments by the simple terms "reading" and
"writing" rather than name them collectively "literacy," because someone who can read and write may still lack the
sensitivity to words that is the essential quality of the literate
man in the broadest sense of literate, while someone else who
can neither read nor write may demonstrate extraordinary
insight into the problems of language. In French, mechanical
knowledge of reading and writing skills is subsumed under
the technical term *alphabétisme,* while *lettré* denotes someone who is awake to the challenge of language. The French
classification is more logical than the English because it distinguishes the technological machinery of literacy from the

essential power that drives it, but the ambiguity of the Anglo-American term can have an advantage if it causes us to recognize implicitly that literacy is always a compound of cultural attitudes and available technologies.

We are accustomed to think of writing as an extension and development of speech itself: whatever I say or think, so long as it is formed in recognizable sounds, can be written down in a formal, more or less accurate way. But writing does not begin as an extension of speech. In its earliest forms, writing competes with speech by creating codes and diagrams that are intended to subvert the need for sound and articulation. All the earliest writing systems are of this type, and while each has its charm and significance, each is in marked ways less efficient than the alphabetic writing developed by the Semites that leads to the Greek and Roman systems of writing.

The most primitive writing systems are attempts to overcome the limitations of speech. A primitive diagram found among the unlettered Ojibwe Indians is actually a letter from a girl to her lover. It provides him with a map to the site of their tryst, thereby solving the difficulty that by speech alone we cannot make plans beyond hailing distance of one another. The oldest known writing system, cuneiform inscriptions dating from about 3000 B.C. in Sumer of Mesopotamia, also defies rather than exploits speech. One cuneiform inscription, preserved on stone tablets, records a cattle sale. The cattle are not indicated by a code to represent the word "cow" or "steer," as in our system; they are represented by signs that depict the cattle themselves. These ideographs enable the writer to bypass speech entirely and deal directly with things. In their earliest forms Egyptian and Chinese writing evaded speech by using hieroglyphs and characters which are written images of the objects notated rather than simple transcriptions of the sounds by which they are normally identified in speech.

Since the Renaissance many wishful students of language have envied these early writing systems precisely because they do sever the connection between speech and notation. Leibniz considered the Chinese characters the prototype for an ideal philosophical system of notation, free of the ambiguities of our spoken language and directly correlated to the objects of thought without the distorting intermediacy of spoken language. For much the same reason, Ezra Pound praised the Chinese system as a paradigm of the poetic medium, because in it the reader immediately sees the thing discussed instead of merely hearing the sounds that represent the thing.

It seems Leibniz and Pound did not fully understand the systems they praised. Early in their development, both Egyptian and Chinese characters soon became inextricably bound to speech, and for obvious reasons. In their primitive forms, hieroglyphs and characters only represented concrete things. Concepts had to be designated by metaphors. In Chinese writing, an ideogram of a woman holding a child represents not only the thing it pictures, but love, and, by extension, the adjective good. Here is ambiguity as plentiful as in speech. Also, there may be as many hieroglyphs or characters in such a writing system as there are phenomena to describe. A full knowledge of written Chinese would demand recognition of some 50,000 characters and compound characters. A rudimentary knowledge demands recognition of at least 500. Consider the difficulty children have in learning the 26 letters of the English alphabet and the Chinese system is revealed in all its cumbersome inefficiency. From the beginning the Egyptians and Chinese recognized the difficulty and introduced into their writing systems elements that made the ideograms correspond to spoken language, and thereby prevented the multiplication of ambiguity and confusion. The Egyptians developed a system of syllabic notation, the Chinese, one of logographs keyed to speech. But even with a phonetic element, these writing systems are difficult. The Egyptian system was swept away by the sparse, practical, and pure alphabetic system, and after many years of cultural resistance, even the Chinese have subscribed to a gradual modification of their written language along Western lines. The importance of such a step cannot be exaggerated. Lenin felt that, when the Western alphabet was introduced into China, it would be the keystone of revolution in the East because the Western writing system would lay the groundwork for the introduction of all Western technologies and ideologies.

Writing begins in competition with speech and then succumbs to the stronger power of the spoken word. Ideographic writing tries to create a new sign language parallel to and distinct from spoken language, but its model for this new language is spoken language itself. It makes much better sense simply to take as the basis of writing the highly developed system of language we already have than to set about creating a new and more primitive system in competition with the existing model. If it's not broken, why fix it? The great technological advances in the use and dissemination of language have been those that exploit speech, not those that compete with it. The alphabet replaced ideograms and logographs; the telephone superseded the telegraph; television begins to outperform print.

The most revolutionary event in the history of writing came with the introduction of signs correlated not with things or ideas or even whole words, but with individual sounds, thereby enabling men easily to transcribe speech. Our alphabet is a product of this revolution, and, in theory at least, an alphabetic system of notation should give a culture access in writing to every form of language manifest in speech. Theory and practice, of course, are quite distinct. No culture has ever written just as it speaks. Speech is often diffuse and incomprehensible divorced from the context of social activity. A literal transcript of a Presidential press conference or a locker-room conversation may make no sense at all to the reader, while a listener present in the room with the speakers would easily understand the words. President Eisenhower's press conferences, reproduced complete with ellipses and a-hems by the *New York Times*, are rambling and incoherent to the reading eye but made some sense when he spoke the words. The give-and-take of the locker room, as with most speech, is seasoned with gesture, slang, dialect, and inflection, all of which the written word usually seeks to purge away in order to reach a generally intelligible product that is both seemly and comprehensible outside of the transient context of human activity.

But writing begins in competition with speech, and even in our alphabetic writing system, the competitive element remains. Writing is not always the obedient handmaiden of spoken language, but seeks a life of its own. This native recalcitrance of writing is obvious in the ideographic and logographic systems of the Orient but is present in all writing systems. Anyone familiar with the written work of American college freshmen knows the disparity between their often fresh conversation and their frequently banal prose. Their talk is lively, they have the power to transpose their words into writing, and yet their writing is tiresome. Writing is a technology of language with a character distinct from the spoken language it pretends to represent.

Neurology offers a partial explanation for this struggle between speech and writing. The ability to write is not confined exactly to those areas of the brain that govern speech. It is possible to suffer brain damage such that the patient cannot speak but can write, or cannot write but can speak. Even the vocabularies of speech and writing may be distinct within the complex of the brain. Most of us use words in writing that never occur in our speech, and vice versa. Learning specialists tell us that the stages by which we acquire writing do not duplicate those by which we learn speech.

Writing is certainly a technology of language, and in our alphabetic system it is intimately allied with speech, but even the most intimate of allies have their separate lives.

Writing has an inherent dignity, born of its challenge to time, that speech does not possess. Where this dignity is abused, it becomes inanity; where it is cultivated, it becomes style. In either event, this *gravitas* is writing's attempt everywhere to distinguish itself from speech. Like rhetoric, writing is more highly organized than speech. What is more, it prides itself on transcending the boundaries of place and time within which speech must be understood. And writing has propriety. Every writing system seems torn by conflicting impulses. On the one hand it wants to include within its scope all the subjects of language itself. Writing means to be the hard copy of human life. But at the same time every writing scheme has its taboos. Much as writing wants to be inclusive, there are some areas of life it either will not or cannot discuss as well as speech. This propriety is clear in traditional and classical civilizations, where certain themes like personal confession are never entertained in writing.

The disparity between speech and writing stems from its dignified attempt to be coherent beyond the limits of time and place. Writing, simply because of this disparity, has often caused alarm when first introduced in a culture. In the first half of the nineteenth century Chief Cobb of the Choctaw tribe denounced the white man for his writing:

> The red man has no books, and when he wants to say what he thinks, he speaks from the mouth, like his fathers before him. He is afraid of writing. When he speaks, he knows what he says. The Great Spirit hears him. Writing is the invention of the palefaces. It gives birth to trouble and fighting. The Great Spirit talks. We hear him in the thunder, in the sound of the wind, and in the water. He never writes.

For Chief Cobb, the difference between speech and writing is essential. For him as for some believers in the Logos doctrine, speech is divine; writing is a false parody of speech subject to manipulation and full of deceit. As his speech shows, the Chief was highly advanced in the art of rhetoric, the first technology of language, but he derided the further technology of written transcription because he believed that, as it transcends speech, it loses the goodness of human discourse.

Chief Cobb will have none of the argument that writing fosters a wider dissemination of opinion and therefore brings mankind closer together: "It gives birth to trouble and fighting." His point is well taken. There can be no assurance that a world where everyone reads and writes will be a better world. Writing lends dignity to the expression of speech but in the process becomes vain and intolerant. Most people who proofread their own writing know the self-gratulatory effect that words on paper have and how hard it is to admit the possibility of error in written statement. Every written word is a kind of incarnation, and many people are all too willing to treat writing as a mystical epiphany when in fact it may only be another avatar of the folly proceeding from the human mouth. When words materialize in writing, they acquire an added presence that often makes criticism more, not less, difficult. Books do not change their minds in light of new evidence, nor is a written sentence liable to empathize with the situation it discusses. To Chief Cobb this hardness of written language defies the plastic power and sympathetic benevolence of the Great Spirit of nature.

Some dreamers have envisioned a world of peace and prosperity built on a foundation of universal language and communication. These visionaries would do well to take Chief Cobb's comments to heart. War can become more likely when men think they understand each other. Understanding never precludes disagreement. When people recognize that they either do not understand or may have misinterpreted someone else's language, they are apt to be politic and patient, but where they believe that the words they hear or read are unambiguous, they will act on them. The language barrier between Moscow and Washington is a great force for peace. It creates in both capitals a doubt about the accuracy of their information. Unless universal language is accompanied by universal good will, the spread of communication arts could mean an increase in the level of world violence.

Writing is not only inflexible because divorced from the living speaker, it also presents thought with deceptive clarity and finality. As long as men disagree about major issues, clarity and finality are invitations to combat, and a more plastic and deferential medium of speech has usually been used where diplomacy seeks to reconcile opposing nations, groups, or individuals. Even in our own print age, the serious conflicts of the world are resolved not by exchanges of diplomatic notes but by private exchange of thought.

In the European tradition, Plato is the most eloquent opponent of writing, and for reasons like Chief Cobb's. Plato, one of the fathers of the Logos doctrine, believes deeply in the ability of language and the dialectic to apprehend the divine reality behind nature. Speech is a vehicle for this apprehension, but writing distorts speech and thwarts our access to real being by corrupting memory. Plato makes Socrates condemn writing in a parable of the *Phaedrus* because if men learn how to use it, "it will implant forgetfulness in their souls: they will cease to exercise memory because they rely on that which is written, calling these things to remembrance no longer from within themselves, but by means of external marks; what you have discovered is a recipe not for memory, but for reminder." Writing destroys memory—this is Plato's argument and the argument of those who today oppose the use of calculators in grade-school mathematics classes. If all problems are soluble by some aid or other, there is an end to memory and reason. Reason is the divine power of ordering and arranging in terms of language. Reason is the method of the Logos, the Word. Writing subverts the Word for Plato, just as in a smaller way the mental activity of the mathematics class is supposed to be stifled when the calculator, not the student, does the problem.

The most curious aspect of Plato's argument, however, is not its logic but its format. The attack on writing is made in a written dialogue (we can be fairly certain that Plato did indeed write, not speak, the *Phaedrus*, intending it for posterity). Here then is a paradox: writing condemned in writing. But this is precisely the situation of all writing. It seeks to encompass the whole world of speech, but at the same time treats this world in its own colder, harder, more distant way. Plato wants the virtues of writing—its permanence, its pretense to objectivity, its calculation, its dignity—but he is unwilling to sacrifice the immediate rapport with the divine element that speech has. Perfectly aware of the contradiction, he presents it in the form of a dialogue, his closest approach to combining the virtues of speech and writing. The *Phaedrus* must be read as it was written—with a sense of humor, a troubled recognition of the gulf between the worlds of speech and writing, and an appreciation of the virtues of both.

ATHENS: WRITING AS A CULTURAL FORCE

Those who have studied the nature of writing have often been intoxicated by the discovery that in certain cultural situations, the exploitation of writing has altered the destiny of civilizations. Taken together, the work of anthropologists like Jack Goody, of media experts like Marshall McLuhan, and of classicists like Eric Havelock, would lead us to believe that writing has altered the way men think; that it has given birth to history, skepticism, and science; that it has changed the political structure of the West. Writing is said to have opened for examination the inner life of man, or on the contrary to have alienated man from himself and the world. Our particular writing system, employing the alphabet, is said to have fathered modern science and technology, and to have been a necessary cause of democracy and the industrial revolution.

All these claims are without foundation. By itself, writing is an inert force. It provokes change only within the living organism of the human community, and the changes it does stimulate make sense only when studied in conjunction with the consciousness of language prevalent in the culture where it is employed.

Those who advance the grandest claims for the revolutionary powers of writing seem to envision cultural history as a kind of physical science. A car traveling along a straight highway at 60 miles per hour that is struck head-on by a truck of twice its weight traveling at 80 miles an hour will undergo a series of rapid and predictable alterations, all of which can be calculated with a fair degree of accuracy from known formulae. The scientific observer, given the right data, knows enough not to be in that car. So some cultural historians have imagined writing to affect societies. Introduce writing, and a more scientific, linear frame of mind ensues. Democracy is made possible. Those who read and write, being more skeptical and industrious, spur a technological upheaval. Writing leads to modern civilization.

In fact, if we must use an analogy, human nature's reaction to a certain kind of chemistry provides a better one. If I buy a bottle of wine, I may store it for a special occasion, I may open it and let it turn to vinegar, or I may christen a boat with it. If I drink it, I may take a sip or polish off the bottle. Depending on my constitution, how much I have eaten, and the time and place, the sip may make me drunk or the whole bottle may affect me no more than a glass of water. If in fact I become inebriated, I might dance on the table or pass out on the floor, again depending on certain factors unique to my body and mind. If I drink the bottle of wine and then don a lampshade, it would be poor logic to say that the alcohol made me a boor. It would be more correct to say that the wine furnished my bad manners with an occasion. Reading and writing, and all the technologies of language, have similar organic properties, and humans use them in similarly complex ways. Their uses and effects vary from individual to individual and from society to society. Writing in itself is not the cause of anything, any more than hydrogen is the cause of water. In certain situations hydrogen becomes part of water. Now water does not exist without hydrogen, but the cause of the water is much larger than the hydrogen molecule itself and can only be understood by examining the complete system of water and environment. Writing by itself does not change the world although in combination with certain other organic forces it might furnish the occasion of change. The chief among these other forces are first the degree and kind of awareness about language existing in the society where writing is used and second the economic structure of that society.

Classical civilization is usually the test case by which students of writing prove their points. How are the technologies of reading and writing related to the rise of the West? Can it be a coincidence that the glories of Greek thought and literature follow so closely on the introduction of the alphabetic writing system?

Before the time of Homer, before the Trojan War, the inhabitants of mainland cities like Mycenae and Pylos in the Peloponnesus had a form of writing now widely known as Linear B. The language behind Linear B, at least in its late phase, was an early form of Greek, while the actual technology for the system seems to have been imported from the eastern Mediterranean. The symbols of Linear B represent individual, spoken syllables.

The most curious thing about Linear B is not what the Greek-speaking peoples of the second millennium B.C. did with it, but what they did not do. They did use it extensively for business and government records, but they hardly seem to have used it at all for literature or religion, even though as traders they must have been familiar with societies where this was the practice. The symbols used in Linear B are more complex than those of the modern alphabet—there are some 80 or 90 basic signs—but not so difficult that knowledge of the system would be beyond the range of ordinary men. Use of Linear B, however, seems to have been monopolized by the managerial classes attached to the palaces of great cities like Mycenae or Pylos. The peoples of the Aegean were by no means backward. Their art, well known for its dolphin designs, and their remarkable Cyclopean architecture are reminders that they had a highly developed culture, yet it was a culture that used the technology of writing in only the most circumscribed way. Linear B was not a magic pill for Mycenean civilization. Its effects were closely tied to whatever notions its users had of the proper role of language in civilized life, and these notions must have been quite distinct from the ideas about language prevailing elsewhere in the Mediterranean world of that era. At any rate, Linear B did not automatically lead to the cultural advances claimed for writing, and whatever inspired the ancestors of Homer and Hesiod is lost to us in the silence that envelops all civilizations that only speak.

After the Dark Age of Greece, from the collapse of Crete to the rise of the Ionian cities, writing disappeared from Greece. Homer refers to writing only once, and then only to tell the story of the messenger whose letter read, "Slay the bearer"—here a letter was necessary for the plot. The *Iliad* and the *Odyssey* were composed and preserved by oral recitation and were probably not written down till after Homer, by which time the Phoenician alphabet had been introduced into the Greek world.

The alphabet, adapted to the idiosyncracies of the Greek language over a period of some four centuries, is a part of but not the cause of a revolution in Western development. The Greek achievement was not the technological one of creating the alphabet; they took it over from the Phoenicians. But while the Phoenicians occupy a remote corner in the history of our civilization, the Attic and Ionic adapters of the alphabet stand at its front because they exploited the technology of alphabetic writing to its fullest. (I use the word Greek to mean the Attic and Ionic segments of Greece that developed the alphabet.) The Phoenicians and some other of their neighbors made an innovation as remarkable as the plow when out of Egyptian writing they developed a system of notation based on the few basic sounds that comprise speech. Having gone so far, they applied this new technology to that dimension of life most important to them— commerce. Alphabetic writing made contracts and business records much easier. So far as we can know, the Phoenicians believed in the inviolability of contracts. Behind a civilization such as this lies a theory of language, rooted in pragmatism, that shuns ambiguity and obfuscation: the business of language is business. Perhaps some similar attitude prevailed in Minoan Crete and Mycenaean Greece, inhibiting the development of writing beyond the counting house.

Nothing better shows how the technologies of literacy are adapted to the styles of various cultures than the contrasting uses that the Phoenicians and the Hebrews made of writing. The Hebrews inherited alphabetic writing from their fellow Semites and neighbors, the Phoenicians. But for them writing was not confined to business but to the service of religion. There is nothing in writing and the alphabet themselves that makes men logical or contemplative, business-like or devout. The alphabetic writing that promoted trade among the children of Baal incited the Hebrews to the study of the law and the prophets.

When the Semitic writing system was imported into Greece around 800 B.C.—there is some reason to think that Cadmus, the legendary inventor of the alphabet, was in fact a Phoenician immigrant to Thebes—it quickly outgrew the bounds of religious and of commercial notation. Cadmus is said to have sown the dragon's teeth that raised a crop of warriors. On Greek soil the alphabet, once established, also bore a mighty crop, one that cannot be explained solely by the technology of alphabetic writing or by improvements in this system made by the Greeks when they refined the signs for vowel sounds. Writing did not make the Greek mind skeptical, logical, historical, or democratic. Instead it furnished an opportunity for these predispositions to flourish. Well before Pericles or even Homer, the Greek-speaking peoples had developed a consciousness of language peculiar to themselves. The work ascribed to Homer is our best but not our only evidence of this literacy. For the Greeks, language was not only for business, or for worship, or for debate, or for humor, though Homer shows us all these uses. Language was also the medium for obtaining what they considered the highest form of human satisfaction, knowledge won by human endeavor and modestly indulged with a joy impervious to the vicissitudes of life. *Hybris*, the word often translated as pride, is the opposite of this satisfaction. It is illiteracy in its most baleful incarnation: the ignorance of the world that comes from not applying the mind to the evidence of language and of the senses leads to pain and destruction. Homer's Agamemnon makes no effort to scrutinize the words of dreams or speeches, and Aeschylus' Agamemnon has the same failing. The evidence of his doom is

all around him in Clytemnestra's irony and Cassandra's ora-
cles if only he will exercise the will to conscious knowledge.
These Agamemnons are full of *hybris;* they are illiterate.

Oedipus, on the other hand, is the literate man as tragic
hero. He is undone not by a fact but by his awareness of one.
Throughout Sophocles' drama, he struggles to understand a
set of words whose meaning, once known, destroys him. His
two greatest feats are exercises in riddle-solving—first the
riddle of the Sphinx, then the Delphic riddle commanding
him to seek the murderer of Laos. Part of Oedipus' heroism
is his willingness, at any cost, to penetrate the veil of language that separates men from appreciating the reality of
their presence in the world. When he finally does appreciate
the relation between language and reality in his own life, he
comes simultaneously to the height of knowledge and the
most bitter consciousness of despair. The demand to wring
sense out of language drives Oedipus and Greek culture. It
is the essence of their literacy.

The Greek tragedies belong to an era long after the introduction of writing, but the consciousness of language that
they exemplify predates it. We can hear it in the Delphic
oracle's ancient love of irony and in Homer's wit. Midas is
told that if he wars on Persia, a mighty nation will be overthrown. Taking this as a favorable omen, he goes to war and
his nation is overthrown. In Homer's poem Odysseus fools
the Cyclops, the prototypical barbarian, by telling him his
name is Nobody, so that when the Cyclops' neighbors ask
who is tormenting him, the monster's reply defeats his expectations. Both these stories depend on an audience alive
to the problems and potentials of language.

A highly developed literacy existed in Greece before the
advent of reading and writing, and once coupled with these
technologies, it shaped classical culture. The foundation of
this literacy was a critical examination of language as the
key to life. Even before they had reading and writing, lan-

guage was for the Greeks a divine medium which it behooved mortals to treat exhaustively and with the greatest diligence. Zeus promised his paramour Semele anything she might name, and then was bound to destroy her in a lightning bolt when she asked for something the meaning of which she did not understand—to know her godly lover in his native form. Here words are inviolable, as in Phoenician contracts, but the stakes are much higher. Life and death are in the power of language.

Of course, language was a life-and-death matter for the Hebrews as well, but not in the same sense as for the Greeks. The difference again is in the basic cultural attitudes toward language. Writing is sometimes said to force a culture to confront the contradictions of its oral tradition and, in resolving them, to become critical. In this view, singers and bards orally pass along the poems and sagas that reflect a culture's history and ideology, adapting their material in each generation to the spirit of the times. Thus the bard makes the memory of his culture anew in each generation. Writing is said to arrest this organic process and fix the traditional lore in whatever incarnation it has at the moment a writing system appears. Once the text is written men may no longer adapt it through the plastic power of oral transmission but must face its apparent contradictions, anachronisms, and barbarisms. In attempting to resolve these anomalies, the new generation of readers and writers becomes critical, skeptical, and self-conscious.

This theory is very attractive but not I think universally true. It explains what happened in Greece because the Greek attitude toward language was critical and self-conscious even before the introduction of the alphabet. It does not explain what happened in Israel because the Hebrew attitude toward language precluded the Greek type of skepticism.

When transcribing the oral versions of Genesis or Job, the Jews included conflicting versions in the written text. In their culture, the mystical properties of language transcended the human order that demands logical consistency in a story. The Judeo-Christian tradition continues the effort begun by the priests of the temple of Solomon to appreciate the paradoxes of the Bible, and many theologians clearly believe that there inheres in language a mystical reality supervening mundane logic. The sublime mystery of the four Hebrew letters that comprise the tetragrammaton representing the name of God is only the best known example of how the faith of the Jewish culture mixed itself inextricably with the technology of the alphabetic writing. The Cabala, which is scrutinized for the hidden significance not only of its syntactical sense but also of its very letters, also proceeds from such a mystical view of language, a view that is nothing if not reverential. But the Greek attitude toward language was very different. First the Greeks improved the alphabet they received from the Semites by systematizing the vowel sounds. It was a technological advance, and more; it was a step the Hebrews, locked into a belief in the immanence of eternal verity within language and writing, would not make. To change the alphabet would be to admit the mortality of the Word, to exalt human industry over divine order. These, however, are precisely the attitudes the Greeks took toward language.

Perhaps the most remarkable feature of the Greek attitude toward language, both before and after the introduction of writing, is its sense of humor. Language for the ancient Greeks is divine and must be scrutinized for truth by every human resource of wisdom and reverence. In this they were not unlike the Jews, but the sense of humor they blended with their reverence distinguishes their consciousness of language from all others. The late Greek word *eutrapelia* summed up for them what the English "sense of humor" conveys. *Eutrapelia* is the spirit of wit and of play, the creative energy of gamesmanship (readers of Kipling will identify the essence of *eutrapelia* in the gusto with which his characters throw themselves into the Game). Almost nothing in the Greek consciousness about language is lugubrious. Even *Oedipus Rex*, the most desolating of the tragedies, leaves one not drained but invigorated by the drama of the Game. Parmenides begins with the verb *to be* and from it deduces that time and space are unreal. Zeno demonstrates with language that Achilles can never beat the tortoise. Theirs are the perennial questions of philosophy, yet everywhere infused with a playful vitality in the use of language that prevents despair and stimulates energy. The most depressing utterances of the Greek tradition are still somehow fresh because of the challenge their language makes to our humanity.

In politics too, this vital literacy was characteristic of the Greek mind, and long before reading and writing. The war councils of the *Iliad* are deliberative bodies in which the man of superior rhetorical skills is likely to prevail and where all the chiefs listen intently to the debate, weighing the validity of the words. The wrath of Achilles is made grander and more monstrous because it exists beyond the persuasion of rhetoric. Passion forces him into seclusion, and passion brings him out. The arguments of Odysseus and Diomedes go for nothing with him. To the Greek mind a man like Achilles, who has divorced himself from the sanctions of language, was an awesome spectacle, and not quite human. Only at the end of the epic, when Achilles is moved by Priam's plea for Hector's body, does he finally rejoin the human community where language prevails, and there the story ends. The combination of reverence and relish for language was inherent in Greek culture and gives Greek literacy its tone.

An example from Athenian history illustrates the distinct flavor of Greek literacy. When the Persians invaded Greece in 480 B.C., part of their navy was manned by Greeks living in the Persian-controlled cities of Ionia. After the defeat at Thermopylae, the Greek navy was forced to withdraw from its position at Artemisium in the face of the Persian advance, but before the ships sailed, Themistocles, the Athenian commander, ordered a message be chiseled in the rocks of the coastline for the Ionian crews to read. In the message he urged them not to aid the Persians in subjugating their fellow Greeks. If you cannot desert the Persian cause, he had written, "at least fight badly." Herodotus, who tells the story, ascribes two motives to Themistocles: "The message might, if the kings did not get to know of it, induce the Ionians to come over to the Greeks, and secondly, if it were reported to Xerxes and made the ground of an accusation against the Ionians, they would be distrusted and not allowed in consequence to take part in engagements at sea."

From this incident it seems clear that the knowledge of reading and writing was widespread in Attic and Ionian culture, for the crews of naval vessels were composed of the lower, so-called naval classes, and Themistocles reckoned that enough of them could read that his message would have effect. The appeal contained in the message on the rocks is honest enough and the occasion was critical—the critical moment for Greek liberty. But even at such a decisive moment, the Attic sense of play and of the ambiguity of language is apparent. Themistocles' message is a ploy, meant to trigger a variety of reactions in the enemy. Here language and its technologies are plastic powers whose proper use leads on to human glory—the glory Themistocles aimed for was victory—and what constitutes a proper use of language is for the ingenuity of the human mind to determine. For the Greeks, language and its technologies were the means of manifesting the supremacy of the mind.

The message at Artemisium shows Greek attitudes toward language in contrast to those of their Asian rivals. What Themistocles did was clever; it is also, even at the distance

of 2500 years, amusing. There is no evidence that the Persian
army had either the skill or the mentality to deploy language
in the same way. The vast majority of Xerxes' men could
neither read nor write, and at least from Herodotus' admittedly biased descriptions, the Persians approached lan-
gauge in a much more inflexible and humorless manner
than the Greeks. Either a man spoke the truth or he spoke
lies. The message in the rocks is an essentially Greek moment in the history of literacy.

Once introduced into Greece, writing soon enhanced the
already existing predisposition of the Greeks to treat language with critical vigor and wit. Cosmological speculations
were already popular in the Greek-speaking world before
writing, as Homer's description of the shield of Achilles at-
tests, but writing permitted these speculations to be freed of
hexameter poetry and to acquire a format all their own. The
alphabetic system spawned lyric and philosophy. In Homer's
world the hexameter line facilitated memory. The hexameter
line is as nearly perfect a vehicle for memorization as the ancient world possessed. Its regular rhythm and, as used by the
early poets, its repetition of stock phrases, allowed for easy
retention in the mind, while its length ensured efficiency by
permitting the greatest possible quantity of information to
be packed into each unit. A shorter poetic line or a less regular meter would have required more work for the memory.
Lyric poetry grows up side by side with the innovation of
prose in the age of writing: the shorter and more irregular
lines of lyric are a poetic luxury of a civilization no longer
needing the rigorous efficiency of hexameter for its cultural
memory. With writing, the hexameter form gradually declined as a means of storing and conveying speculative and
purely informative materials and was slowly replaced by
prose, in which there is more range for refinement of thought
and more leeway for precision unencumbered by the necessity of meter. Most of the pre-Socratic philosophers wrote

in verse—often very bad verse—presumably in order to cast their thought in memorable form. Plato made prose the vehicle for philosophy and thereby caused a revolution.

But if writing and prose gradually replaced oral recitation and poetry as the official means of cultural record, they nevertheless did not change the central role of the spoken word in Greek life. By the time of Herodotus and Thucydides in the fifth century, history had been reduced to prose and a civilized Athenian considered the *Iliad* a poor factual record of the past, no matter how grand a poem. But Herodotus and Thucydides, for all that they worked in written prose, were still citizens of a culture that gave the highest eminence to rhetoric. The gist of the *Histories* and *The Peloponnesian Wars* is contained in the speeches each author reconstructs, often from memory—his own or others'. For these men writing did not replace oral culture but examined it more closely. Close examination, moreover, was nothing new—the impulse to scrutinize language for the better appreciation of life was the legacy of the heroes of the *Iliad* and of the clients of Apollo at Delphi.

Greeks who learned how to read and write did not then forget oral record. Some of the Athenian soldiers captured at Syracuse in 413, by which time reading and writing skills had long been generally disseminated in the population, saved themselves from slavery by reciting whole passages of Euripides for their captors. If writing does supplant memory of oral tradition, it did so slowly in Athens. But in fact writing only drives out memory in a culture that has lost its love for the spoken word—a description that may suit our culture but not that of Athens at any time in the classical period.

I have so far treated reading and writing together, though they are obviously separate operations. Reading is a distinct operation emphasizing the use of the eye, not the hand. Reading is generally easier to learn than writing, and until our century, many more people knew how to read than write.

In the ancient world, the diffusion of writing was limited by the time and materials requisite to the skill. In many cultures the actual process of writing was complex, costly, and restricted to professionally trained scribal classes who studied the formation of letters, the preparation of inks, and the manipulation of styluses, as well as correct grammar and proper form. Reading, on the other hand, requires only a trained eye and a piece of writing, which need not even be purchased. The only investment necessary for reading is in time and money for learning the skill.

"He can't read, he can't swim" was an Athenian catchphrase in the fifth century, denoting a man without the basic social skills. Themistocles expected the Ionian crews at Artemesium to be able to read, but it is doubtful many of them could write—or write correctly. The graffiti of antiquity are often misspelled and ungrammatical, and those of Athens are no exception. In the fifth century, when they were able to nominate one candidate a year for ostracism, the Athenians indulged this privilege by writing the name of their choice on broken shards of pottery called *ostraka*, whence the name of the election. Many of these survive. Some seem to have been prepared en masse for those citizens unable or unwilling to write the name out themselves. In an age when the skills of literacy were supposedly widespread, Aristides, then a leading candidate for expulsion, wrote his own name on an *ostrakon* for a voter who could not himself write. The *ostraka* surviving from an ostracism vote on Themistocles show his name spelled in a variety of ways: Themistoclees, Themisthclees, Themisthoclkeies, Themsthocles. The skill of reading was undoubtedly more highly developed and widely diffused than that of writing.

At least initially, reading is closely connected with oral culture. The reader, whether alone or in a group, speaks the written words aloud. In societies that have recently adopted reading, the normal procedure, apparently, is to read in groups, as in the old oral system of transmission, with one man taking the role of reciter while the others listen. In our own culture, many texts, like newspapers, novels, and the Bible, were read aloud in the family circle right into this century. In such societies, even when men read alone, they speak the words aloud to themselves. Silent reading is a fairly recent refinement. In the early history of the skill, the communal aspect of reading makes writing available to much larger audiences, since only one skilled reader is required to pass along the written information to a large group. Reading aloud maintains continuity between the old oral culture and the new society of written texts.

At first glance, reading seems like the passive incarnation of the dynamic process of writing. The writer creates. He actively transmits words. The reader merely receives. But reading can be either mechanical or dynamic, depending on the mind of the reader and, more particularly, on the mental endowments with which he meets the challenge of language.

It seems clear that reading has no necessary characteristics of passivity; however, some have claimed that it possesses an inherent tendency to make men more conscious of themselves as individuals. In this theory, reading evolves from communal recitation to private confrontation of a text. Soon the words of the text are not spoken aloud. By the end of the fifth century, Athens produced its first reference to men reading alone. The text, so it is said, then spoke to the reader as an individual, not as a member of a group, and his dialogue with the written word developed his sense of self. The reader becomes conscious that the text exists for him as it does for no one else because no one else shares exactly his experience of understanding it. His reading both develops his sense of self and begins to isolate him from other men, as he would not be isolated if he received his cultural information by oral recitation.

The first mention of the solitary reader is in Aristophanes' *Frogs*, where the god Dionysos announces that he has been overcome by admiration of Euripides "while sitting on the deck one day reading the *Andromeda* to myself." The exemplar of reading as a means to self-awareness would be Faust, alone in his chamber, absorbing the accumulated wisdom of the Western tradition until his sense of self can no longer be accommodated in the human community. Faust has literally read himself out of the human race. He becomes the archetype of modern man, individual but isolated, searching for some way to employ his reading in the fulfillment of his ever-expanding self-interest. Reading thus contains, according to this thesis, the germ of both Western man's recognition of supreme selfhood and of his tragic self-absorption.

It is true that once reading becomes the vehicle for the transmission of culture, the need to assemble the population in masses for oral recitation begins to decline, but it does not follow that reading compels men to become isolated in their selfhood. Classical civilization attained wide dissemination of the skills of reading and writing—at least as wide as that of Germany or England in the sixteenth century—but it was Northern Europe that produced the Faust legend. The ancient world has nothing comparable. Men who know their culture by oral transmission may yet think as critical individuals, and, conversely, those who have been reared on the written text may act like sheep. The *Odyssey* is an epic of the oral age, but Telemachus nonetheless develops a sense of self. For training in self-reliance and individual consciousness, I would rather trust Homer's oral education than the book learning that produced the main culture of Hitler's Germany.

Like the other technologies of language, from which it is distinct in many ways, reading has few inborn powers. It acquires its dynamic from the ideological framework in which it is deployed.

SPARTA AND FEAR OF WRITING

I have been using the word Greek indiscriminately to indicate those city-states that wedded the technology of writing with the productive élan that characterizes for us the
classical world in its glory. But conditions were not right for
the development of writing in all the Greek states. Sparta is
the preeminent example. The Spartans received writing at
about the same time as the rest of Greece. Like Athens, they
had a strong economy and a noble tradition. Writing, however, was never more than a practical tool of business—almost
a necessary evil of communication—among the Spartans. Plutarch says that the legendary Lycurgus, whose edicts reflect
Spartan policy in the sixth century, forbade writing,

> for he thought that if the most important and binding
> principles which conduce to the prosperity and virtue of
> a city were implanted in the habits and training of its citi-
> zens, they would remain unchanged and secure, having a
> stronger bond than compulsion in the fixed purposes im-
> parted to the young by education, which performs the of-
> fice of a law-giver for every one of them. And as for minor
> matters such as business contracts, and cases where the
> needs vary from time to time, it was better, as he thought,
> not to hamper them by written constraints of fixed usages,
> but to suffer them, as occasion demanded, to reach such
> modifications as educated men should determine. Indeed
> he assigned the function of law-making wholly and en-
> tirely to education.

The Lycurgus of legend was no philistine; he opposed
writing because he loved education. For Lycurgus, writing
subverted the state by making law external and inflexible.
When it is written down, citizens no longer understand the
law; they merely obey it. Plutarch notes that the loss in business efficiency resulting from a ban upon writing was to
Lycurgus minor compared to the gain in flexibility and good
sense. A modern historian confirms that, while the Spartan

upper classes certainly knew how to read and write, probably from 600 B.C. onwards, the society made little inventive
use of the technology except as required by votive inscriptions and diplomatic exchanges. Our term laconic is derived
from the Greek adjective for Sparta; it fits. The Spartan approach to writing was laconic in the extreme, while a hundred miles away the Athenians had invested this technology
with all the inventive play of their culture.

The Spartan reticence about the use of writing results
from their general approach to language, about which Plutarch's remarks have already provided a clue. Education for
the Spartan was only secondarily about language; foremost
it was training in the habits of good citizenship. If everyone
behaved in the correct manner, what need would there be
for written laws? And if the actions of the citizen body as a
whole were a living manual of conduct, why bother to appeal to the page for further instruction? The Spartan ideal
glorifies action and views language arts warily. Even in rhetoric the Spartan goal was to speak plainly and reveal one's
thinking in deeds.

Writing is no guarantee of cultural superiority. The long
history of its praise in the Western tradition is the self-
interested product of those who write, but there has always
been a party, less audible by the nature of its doctrine, opposed to writing. The Spartan believed that the unrecorded
good behavior of citizens, though lost to history, was worth
a book full of unrealized ideals. Gray's *Elegy* reminds us that
the lot of the illiterate peasant not only circumscribed "their
growing virtues, but their crimes confined." Today, the resistance of American students to the blandishments of an educational curriculum that stresses writing is a reminder that
the opposition party still has a constituency. Moreover, we
cannot be sure that the view antagonistic to writing is inherently inferior. Let it be noted that in the contest between
Sparta and Athens, the antagonist prevailed.

Writing gives no assurance of cultural superiority, and in fact brings with it the potential for alienation and cultural anxiety, twin evils that befell Greek civilization in the Alexandrian period. By the third and second centuries, reading and writing had produced at Alexandria a culture that could support a great library and a host of scholars. The literature of this period is chiefly remembered for its idylls, a term for us full of pastoral associations, but the real countryside of which the poets sang—Sicily or Arcadia or the lesser islands— consisted of poor farming communities where the skills of reading and writing were largely uncultivated. Up to the Alexandrian period, civilized men regarded these outposts as uncouth and unlettered. Then the Alexandrians idealized them into pastoral wonderlands precisely because they were unlettered. There the shepherd still sang to his beloved and carried on the simple ways of an earlier period before the advent of writing—or so at least the Hellenistic scholar-poets imagined. To portray this golden world of pre-technological virtues, Theocritus—and Vergil after him—employed the hexameters that had fallen into disuse with the rise of writing and prose.

The message of Alexandrian culture, which is nothing if not a product of reading and writing, is one of weariness with the very technologies that created it. Surrounded by papyrus and parchment, the Hellenistic scholars looked back to the pre-alphabetic world of Homer with affection and a touch of envy. These guardians of the written text were themselves victims of the peculiar dialectic that reading and writing set in motion within classical civilization. Once reading and writing had been introduced, their uses were largely determined by the existing economic and ideological structures of the Greek communities. These structures were then influenced by the new technologies reciprocally. This reciprocal process is organic and complex. In it, cause and effect are almost inextricably joined. Every culture exposed to new technologies of language will produce a different amalgam, depending on the type of technology introduced and the existing social situation. In the case of Greek culture, the technology of writing took root in a society alive to language as a challenge that, once met, fulfilled its highest expectation of human endeavor. By the time of Alexander writing had attained a dizzy eminence among the cultural skills known to the Greeks. The written word had come to represent the fullness of life for many Greeks, and Alexander carried his copy of the *Iliad* to the banks of the Indus in a treasure chest.

Even as writing came to epitomize the glory of human experience, however, it became increasingly a symbol of the way in which technological man is alienated from the living world to which his technologies supposedly give him access. The worker on the Detroit assembly line sees his labor embodied in car after duplicate car over whose design and marketing he has no control, and loses his sense of personal dignity. The purchaser of the car, surrounded by concrete and metal, is alienated from the natural world that the car is designed to make more accessible. Likewise the Alexandrian writer was alienated from language itself, and because language is everyone's means of knowing the relation between himself and the world, he was alienated from knowledge. In speech a man may clarify, debate, explain, and correct himself; in writing the author rarely has these opportunities with his audience. What is written leaves him, and what is written is never an adequate realization of that part of the world it discusses. Man the writer sees his life ebbing away in a stream of imperfect actualizations. Each piece of writing merely reinforces the feeling that language is no longer a fluid connection with reality but instead a kind of imperfect eulogy for thoughts, events, and passions that never captures the wholeness of the thing written about. Fully developed, writing reminds us that it is only a parody, and the society that thoroughly adapts itself to writing runs the risk, as Chief Cobb and Plato point out, of having less, not more, rapport with the world which it had sought to embrace in the very act of writing.

In our day, the college freshman contemplates his prose with bored detachment. The businessman inflicts pain in all directions, not least on himself, by his bone-crushing jargon. Writing has become a burden, a chore. Writing ought to transcribe the vitality of our culture. Instead it reflects our ennui. We are victims of the same alienation that first afflicted the bookmen of Alexandria.

CHAPTER THREE

Word against Empire: Literacy and Power

In early Latin, well before Cicero's time, *litteratus* meant to be branded with a letter of the alphabet—for the Roman forefathers a mark of slavery. The procedure epitomizes the use of writing as a means of power. Like every other technology, writing can be exploited. The businessman profits by superior records and written contracts; the warrior prevails because of accurate communications; the priest monopolizes knowledge of the sacred text; and the lawyer develops a written code decipherable only by the elect. Every society, and perhaps most individuals, will try to use whatever literacy they have to advantage. Literacy always has an aspect of power.

Claude Lévi-Strauss asserts that the introduction of writing is invariably followed by a consolidation of power in the hands of an authoritarian elite. Like the Alexandrian scholars before him, he looks back to a happier time before writing, a time for the French anthropologist not Homeric but primitive. His observation is not a law of life but a judgment on the greater Latin culture of which he himself is a part. Ancient history provides numerous examples that refute him. In parts of Greece knowledge of reading and writing combined with existing economies to produce democratic revolutions. It seems probable that the first elements of the Athenian population that learned reading and writing were the businessmen and traders. The commercial advantage they gained by the new technology made them first more prosperous, then more politically assertive. In the century before Pericles the wealth of Athens, assisted by the technology of writing, facilitated the enfranchisement first of the middle classes and then of all free men. Aristocrats like Plato were ambivalent about the new technology. In Athens it is probable that the appearance of writing meant a gain in power for the free community as a whole and did not promote a power grab by any new elite. Writing always increases the power at the disposal of a civilization, but who wields this power toward what ends is a cultural variable. This chapter examines the confrontation of two literacies in the ancient world—the literacy of the pagan state and the literacy of the Church—as a test case of the way literacy becomes power.

ROME: UNIVERSAL LANGUAGE
AND WORLD DOMINATION

The Roman state provides the clearest example of writing in the service of authority. Polybius, who in the second century B.C. recorded the history of Rome's rise to world power, makes it clear that a knowledge of writing was requisite for service in the citizen army of the day, where written watchwords and orders were universally in use. Judging by the graffiti at Pompeii, a knowledge of reading and writing was well established among all the social orders of that resort city. Bakers and other tradesmen are well represented on the walls there, as are lower-class exhortations of local sporting teams. There are no accurate figures for comparison, but it is not outrageous to guess that more Italians could read and write in the first century of the Christian era than could in the nineteenth. As late as 1900, 33 percent of the recruits in the Italian army were classified as illiterate; twenty years earlier the rate had been 50 percent. Almost certainly the number of those without reading or writing skills would have been less in the army of the Caesars. In the first century A.D. Martial boasted that amid the Celtic frosts the stern centurion flipped through his pages. He was probably not exaggerating.

The Romans quickly adapted writing to the prevailing genius of their civilization—social organization. Written orders and passwords eliminated confusion in the military ranks; records and memoranda greatly enhanced the efficiency of the bureaucracy necessary to run an empire. Egypt had known the value of writing as a tool of social organization, but there, knowledge of writing had been restricted to the ruling religious and political elites. An Egyptian hymn in praise of learning celebrates the elitist role of letters: "Love letters as your mother. You may protect yourself from hard labor of any kind and be a magistrate of high repute." In Egypt writing made an accommodation with the existing hierarchical social order, with the result that a small segment of the population used it to exploit the masses. A culture like Egypt's behaves as Lévi-Strauss anticipates. Writing becomes a tool of authoritarianism, and its dissemination is rigorously controlled by those in power, who fear for their positions if the skill should become commonplace. The authoritarian assumes that, once they have learned to read and write, his subjects will therefore become critical and competitive. He guards the skill of writing as he guards his power.

The Romans, however, possessed an easier alphabet and a cannier sense of power than the Egyptians, and they engineered a system of mass reading and writing skills. At Rome, the knowledge of letters was widely diffused, with the same result as in Egypt, only better secured. A large and varied population of readers and writers allows for the formation of broadly based bureaucracies and assures a pool of potential managerial talent drawn from a variety of classes, and thereby social stability is promoted. The army corporal who can read and write does not threaten his rulers simply because he possesses these skills; he is in fact a more efficient and obedient soldier for them. What is crucial is that he be trained not only to read and write but to obey what he reads and to write according to the method approved by his superiors. The skills of reading and writing have no inherent disposition to produce independent thinking. This talent grows not from technologies of language but from attitudes toward language itself. Reading and writing may in some circumstances facilitate an independent, critical spirit, but they are not its cause.

The general dissemination of reading and writing helped hold the Roman empire together as surely as did its roads. The business of the state required written documents for its smooth execution. What is more, it demanded a universal language everywhere written and understood according to set rules. The language was Latin and the rules those of the grammarians, enunciated from the second century B.C. onward. In a famous story, Suetonius relates that the emperor Augustus, who was himself eccentric in his spelling (his writing was sometimes phonetic, says Suetonius, at other times merely sloppy), once cashiered a consular governor for being *rudis et indoctus,* "backward and ignorant," because the official couldn't spell in the proper style. The offending gentleman had written *ixi* for *ipsi.* Augustus was no petty tyrant but a brilliant administrator of the world's largest bureaucracy. An emperor may write as he pleases, but a functionary must perform according to form.

Proper form has three functions in the development of writing. It discourages ambiguity; it instills a sense of discipline in the user; and it favors the natural inclination of writing systems toward propriety.

Uniform grammar and spelling go a long way toward

eliminating confusion in communication and are therefore much prized in any bureaucracy. Contemplate the confusion that results in the attempt to assemble a do-it-yourself product from directions written by Formosans or the potential damage that might ensue when in a military manual the words "The missile's trigger short-circuits when launched manually" are written "The missiles trigger short-circuits when launched manually." In the context of Latin civilization, and of our own, it is not enough to know how to read and write; the state insists that one know how to do these according to a uniform standard of correct form, and the punishment for those who do not is exclusion from its munificence, a severe penalty where the state itself is the chief employer.

The teaching of correct written form has for the state the collateral advantage that, besides creating a generally intelligible medium of communication free of ambiguity, it inspires in the learner respect for authority. The ideal bureaucrat or soldier will not only spell well but will acknowledge the competence of a dictionary. His training has not only the practical application of good spelling but the more formidable result of instilling in him a sense of regularity and obedience.

We must be very careful in drawing any conclusion from the fact that writing is a method of social discipline. So for that matter is learning to drive. Society and individuals alike have a legitimate interest in devising codes of behavior that facilitate rapid and intelligible communication. It does not follow that writing is in itself elitist or authoritarian any more than the rules of the road are. In some cultures the code of correct writing will be suited to the needs of the largest possible numbers. In others it will be rigged against them. Once again, the determining factors will be attitudes toward language, available technologies, and economic realities. At Rome the quality of literacy initially dictated that reading and writing skills be widely diffused among the population in order to promote social efficiency and political conquest. Later, in response to the demands of empire, these skills became basic tools of the organization of the world state. But curiously enough, the very pressures that encouraged the spread of writing among the population also militated for the development of a strict code of correct usage, which in turn became a barrier between the population and the written language as this code grew to be complex and stagnant. The empire needed a correct, written language to rule the world, but the more correct it became, the less it had to do with the world it governed.

By the time of Augustus, every schoolboy knew that certain forms of Latin represented the correct way to deploy the written language. Vergil, Ovid, and Lucretius were well known to all classes. Then and now students of Latin looked to these poets, and their counterparts in prose—Cicero, Caesar, Livy—as models of how Latin ought to be written. For a moment in the history of the Roman republic the formal written language must have reflected the actual state of good spoken Latin, but even in Vergil's time the written and the spoken language had begun to diverge. In time this divergence would lead to the evolution of the romance languages, and that development in part stemmed from the quality of literacy in the early empire. The business of the state required a dependable universal language unsullied by the vagaries of popular speech, while the business of life continued to be conducted in a changing, lively Latin increasingly removed from the codes of correct writing mandated for official communication.

Different conventions for written and spoken Latin had their roots not only in the special Roman situation, but perhaps in the nature of writing itself. Even as it seeks to perform all the feats of speech, writing maintains its sense of propriety. Unlike speech, writing is not rooted in the individual moment or place. Writing reaches beyond time and place to those out of earshot. It attempts to purge itself of the ephemera of oral communication. The progress of Greek literature furnishes an example of how a separate written language can grow out of a highly developed culture. The great works of fifth-century Athens were still somehow connected to speech. The drama was sung and spoken; the poetry sung and chanted; the histories largely recorded rhetoric; Plato writes dialogues; and what we have of Aristotle is his students' lecture notes. By the time the library flourished at Alexandria in the third century, however, two languages had developed, one written and one spoken. The written language was by then produced according to canons that began to be formulated among the scholars of that city. The poetry, often pastoral and usually idiosyncratic, was nonetheless artificial and meant to be read.

As it began its expansion, Rome also began to develop formal, written Latin for the business of empire. The soldier and the grammarian proceeded in lockstep to spread the Roman way, one by conquering the world, the other by providing it with correct Latin as a medium of organization.

The formulation of socially approved rules and conventions of language is a formidable development in the life of a culture. Language is the medium by which we register and exercise our knowledge of the world, and attempts to formalize language are attempts to regulate this knowledge. The structure we impose on words in part mirrors and in part dictates how we perceive the world. He who sets the rules of usage shapes ideology. In many senses, every dictionary or handbook of grammar is a political document, dictating the permissible structures of reality. The scholars of Alexandria picked through the corpus of Homer for lines they considered spurious because of their lack of propriety. "It is improper for Agamemnon to make such remarks," reads the scholiast on one manuscript, showing his sense of decorum. Once language has been systematized in a written code, even blind Homer may be censured. Homer's language closely reflects the speech of his time, but 500 years later dual codes of propriety had developed, one for written and another for spoken discourse. The codes of written propriety increasingly excluded what would have been natural, spoken language for Homer. As the written language is gradually reduced to a formal system, as Greek was first in Athens and later in Alexandria and as Latin was by the time of the Antonines in the second century A.D., the world of speech becomes increasingly more remote from the written discourse of bureaucrat, poet, or philosopher. The widening gap is indicative of a split in the mentality of the afflicted civilization.

In the ancient world this split manifested itself in any number of ways—the graffiti of Pompeii juxtapose quotations from Vergil with snatches of popular songs, the official next to the popular tongue. The triumph of Christianity, however, reveals the full consequences to a civilization that evolves conflicting systems of literacy. Christianity sponsored a new literacy as well as a new faith, and we still live in the wake of the upheaval that occurred when the literacy of Rome collided with the literacy of the Word.

By the first century B.C., the ancient world had replaced the old coalition between speech and writing with twin but increasingly unrelated systems of correct writing and rhetoric on the one hand and popular oral culture on the other. The official system demanded not only training in the basic skills of reading and writing but knowledge of the written tradition, of correct orthography, and of proper rhetorical style. However, each advance in the systematic presentation of a language increases the distance between the official tongue and the reality of speech. Both Petronius in the first century and Augustine in the fourth were quick to note the disparity between rhetoric and life. For both of them, rhetoric had evolved so far from the art practiced by Thucydides'

Athenians or Livy's Romans that it represented only hollow bombast. In the *Satyricon*, Petronius' hypocrites aspire to the most correct formal Latin, while they lead their lives according to the language of the streets. For Augustine the gap between the empty forms of rhetoric and the spontaneous emotions of ordinary speech epitomized the alienation of the world from God. His *Confessions* is an attempt to unite the vigor of the Latin language used in daily life with the formal conceits of correct rhetoric.

THE REVOLUTIONARY LITERACY OF THE CHURCH

From the beginning Christianity was the religion of the popular, spoken language. The early Church opposed the formal systems of written and rhetorical language because, consciously or not, it recognized that a world perceived through the medium of the stylized language of the bureaucracy or the polished rhetoric of the scholars and law courts could never be a Christian world. The literacy of the empire was compounded of a variety of elements, against all of which the Church set itself. The official written Latin of the bureaucracy had evolved from the economic and political pressures of empire. It had become a language of political domination, and the Church was bound to oppose it, just as it opposed the ideology in whose service that language was employed. School-taught rhetoric modelled itself on the image of a Greek oratory already old, remote, and ideologically suspect. The Church could as easily live with pagan mythology as with pagan rhetoric. The best Latin and the best Greek were increasingly available only to those who were born to them or could afford to be trained in them. As a populist movement, the early Church necessarily opposed the elitist bent of classical literacy. The early Church resisted, and finally replaced the literacy of the ancient world.

For a short while Christianity avoided writing altogether. The gospels were not reduced to writing till some thirty to sixty years after the death of Jesus, partly because the Christian community anticipated the imminent dissolution of the created world and therefore saw no need to preserve the sacred texts, but partly because the new religion distrusted the whole nexus of ideology and technology represented by the official written language of the empire. When the Church did condescend to transcribe its tradition, it invented a new medium, the codex, to replace the scroll associated with the established literacy it sought to replace. Early Christianity was a reaction against the official written culture of the Greco-Roman world, and it harked back to an oral society like Homer's. In an oral society there is no gulf between the language of life and the language of power; one is a refinement of the other. So it was for the Christian. Jesus himself, like Socrates, had written nothing except when pressed by the scribes and Pharisees to comment on the Mosaic law that condemned the woman taken in adultery. On this occasion, Jesus is said to have written in the dust. He then replied, "Let him who is without sin cast the first stone." His curious behavior may have been a deliberate parody of the literacy of the scribes and Pharisees—as much as to say, "Your written law is only dust."

A similar contempt for the formal apparatus of literacy marks the first Christian centuries. The Acts of the Apostles relates with a certain amount of pride that the apostles Peter and John were accounted *agrammatoi* and *idiotai*, "unlettered and uncouth," by the habitués of the temple at Jerusalem. The adjectives are the Greek equivalent of *rudis et indoctus*, the qualities for which Augustus cashiered his consular officer. The sins of the bureaucracy were the virtues of the faithful. Summing up the history of the Church from the third century, Origen wrote that the only reasonable explanation of the apostles' success in establishing a Christian community was that "the apostles of Jesus, unlettered and uncouth men"—Origen is consciously quoting the book of Acts—"based their mandate to proclaim Christianity to men on nothing but the power given to them and on grace inherent in the Word for revealing the truth in things." Tacitus in the second century and the heretic emperor Julian in the fourth shared Origen's appraisal of the Christians as uncouth and unlettered, but for these good Romans, bred in the established literacy, the observation was not a compliment. Julian, the last pagan emperor, denounced the Christians through pages of diatribe for their ignorance of the great classical texts. But that ignorance was a point of pride with his opponents. They had thrown off the shackles of the official language of the pagan world and subscribed to a more genuine, oral tradition firmly rooted both in the common speech of men, and beyond that, in the Word of God, celebrated in the Logos doctrine of the fourth gospel. Papias, the bishop of Hierapolis around A.D. 130, sought out men who had known or seen Jesus and his followers because, he is reputed to have said, "I did not suppose that what I got from books would help me as much as the living, surviving voice." When the witnesses of Jesus' ministry began to die off and a written record was necessary to preserve the tradition, the language employed was not official Latin or literary Greek, but the *koine*, the common Greek spoken in daily life by the peoples of the eastern Mediterrean.

Christianity is sometimes called a religion of the book because its traditions and doctrines are embodied in a text, but in fact this religion of the book devalued the skills of reading and writing. Christianity sought to propagate not the book, but the Word, and a few priestly readers could accomplish this as well as a population universally trained in the mechanics of literacy. The collapse of mass reading and writing skills in the late Empire and their abeyance during the period from roughly 500 to 1000 are generally regarded as

symptoms of the fall of Western culture into an age of unreflecting illiteracy. This view is wrong on two accounts. The
so-called Dark Ages were neither unreflecting nor illiterate.
The absence in this period of widespread reading and writing
skills such as had existed under Trajan in the second century
was a foreseeable result of the early Christian attitude toward the prevailing literacy of the classical world. It was, in
part, the result cultivated by the Church, which sponsored a
new form of literacy based less on written texts and formalized language and more on the spoken word and the common
tongue.

In our own day we have marvelled at the excesses of
revolutionary governments like that of Communist China,
which has attempted to "reeducate" an entire population.
The Christian attack on classical literacy was part of the im-
plementation of a similarly revolutionary program, by which
the Church hoped that the population of the ancient world
would break their ties to the old gods, the old bureaucracy,
and the old politics, all of which were tied to the old literacy
of official and literary texts. Gibbon, still the best chronicler
of the confrontation between Church and classical civilization, presents the advent of Christianity as cultural upheaval
that influenced—Gibbon would have said infected—every aspect of classical life. Gibbon believed that even in his own
day the world had not fully recovered from what he considered the crippling effects of Christianity. The evidence about
literacy in the ancient world seems to support Gibbon's views
and shows in miniature the cultural revolution he described
in *The Decline and Fall.*

At heart, the Church's quarrel with the empire was a
confrontation of two opposed attitudes toward language.
Cultivated speakers of Latin and Greek, on the one hand,
had evolved a highly formal literacy that provided the basis
of education and of power. This literacy was increasingly
stylized, on the Alexandrian model, and as it became artificial, it also became exclusive. With time, the Platonic notion

that ultimate truth somehow resided in language, and most especially in the spoken word, was badly eroded by the realities of political life. Language more and more became a pragmatic medium of organization without reference to any metaphysical precepts whatsoever, and where language was still thought to house truth, the dogma of the time held that this truth was accessible only to those who had mastered the requisite skills of reading and writing and the correct forms for deploying them. Against this ever more rigid attitude toward language, the Church offered a new variety of literacy in which the fundamental sanctity of spoken language was reaffirmed (in this at least the Christian movement was reactionary more than revolutionary) and the idea of correct usage was temporarily discarded. In the Christian scheme, truth once again inhered in the Word, and the truth once again was available to all who had the spirit to listen in faith: "He that hath ears, let him hear," Jesus had said, stressing the ear over the eye. It was a dictum the Church lived by.

By the fifth century the Christian program had triumphed, and victory brought paradox, for the Church in succeeding the ancient regime assumed its authority. But that authority was best exercised through the old system of bureaucracies, and these bureaucracies functioned best with standardized, written, and formal language, the backbone of the literacy against which the Church had been engaged. Like all successful revolutionaries, the churchmen found themselves suddenly created in the image of the tyrants they had displaced. Their solution to the conundrum of literacy was a compromise that preserved both the new power and the traditional ideology of the Church. The official, written literacy of the old empire was maintained as a means of organizing the business of Europe and the Church, but knowledge of it was restricted to those who were doctrinally sound and therefore not liable to contamination—in other words, the churchmen themselves.

Like the Egyptian and Hebrew priestly classes before them, the Christian churchmen kept a monopoly on written literacy, with far-reaching consequences for European civilization. Initially, writing gave the Church effective control over all social institutions, even monarchies, since these depended upon the priestly, scribal classes for the paperwork necessary to the development of stable, centralized organizations. Among the clergy, instructions could readily and intelligibly pass in written Latin, but at all other levels of civil society, such easy communication was never assumed. The medieval kings of England, for instance, were commonly unable to write and had to hire readers. Thus the mobilization of European society for the crusades was undertaken by the only body capable of an act of such broad organization, the literate Church. No secular institution existed with the capacity for handling the logistics of an enterprise as detailed as the crusades, an undertaking that would require records and communication such as only the Church could muster. And as the crusades became secularized, they failed. Here as throughout history, literacy underwrites the endeavors of civilization in fundamental ways.

But while the new Christian literacy had the desirable effect of consolidating power in the hands of the clergy, the Church did not undertake it merely as a means to power. It was also ideologically necessary for the Church to promote it. Early Christian literacy had its origins in speech and oral tradition. Its commitment to speech and the common language of men was meant to manifest the Logos. Christianity was to be a religion of the ear, not the eye. The ear, as Plato and Chief Cobb felt, is a surer judge of truth; speech is the image of the divine essence of language, and formal, written literacy is a corruption of pure Logos. For Gregory of Tours, or Pope Gregory, both writing in the sixth century, this revolutionary ideology is still a quickening force. Gregory of Tours, himself a skilled rhetorician, writes,

I fear that when I begin to write, since I am without learning in rhetoric and the art of grammar, the learned will say to me, "Uncouth and ignorant man, what makes you think that this gives you a place among writers? How do you suppose critics will receive this work, which is neither provided with artistic skill nor helped out by any knowledge of letters? You who have no useful foundation in letters, who do not know how to distinguish between nouns, who often put feminines for masculines, neuters for feminines, and masculines for neuters; who often, furthermore, do not put even prepositions in the place where the authority of the more celebrated mentors has decreed they belong." . . . I shall reply to them saying, "I do the same work as you and by my very roughness will provide matter for your skill."

The bishop of Tours was an accomplished stylist, and his protestations of rhetorical insufficiency must be taken with a grain of salt, yet he is perfectly serious in asserting that for the good Christian the truth is not found in decorum—the "authority of the more celebrated mentors"—but in "my very roughness." Gregory the Great spoke in the same tradition as did the bishop of Tours when he rejected decorum in language: "I despise the proper constructions and cases, because I think it very unfitting that the words of the celestial oracle should be restricted by the rules of Donatus." Donatus of the fourth and Priscian of the sixth Christian century were the established Latin grammatical authorities on correct use of language. Even today they influence our grammars, and the conflict between spontaneity and decorum continues.

FORMAL AND VERNACULAR
LITERACY IN THE MIDDLE AGES

The Church faced obvious problems in its ideological commitment to the preservation of a revolutionary, oral form of literacy. First, the Church itself had to maintain a correct, written standard of language for its business. Gregory of Tours and Pope Gregory themselves both wrote their formal letters and treatises in precise Latin. Decorum was essential to clarity and efficiency, and hence to power. But the Church's ideology was also undermined by the growing mutual unintelligibility of spoken Latin as the vernacular European languages evolved from it. This degeneration of the spoken language into various distinct new tongues was itself fostered by the existence of a strict standard of propriety for the written language. A formal standard for written expression may assure efficiency in official communication, but it also creates a rigid system of language that soon loses rapport with the ever-changing forms of speech in which the business of life is largely conducted.

By the end of the first Christian centuries the split between the formal literacy of power and the vernacular literacy of daily life was an immediate problem for the West. In the eighth century, a Bavarian priest baptized a child *"in nomine patria et filia et spiritu sancta"*—that is, "in the name of the fatherland, the daughter, and the holy spiritess." Pope Zackary, acting in the ideological spirit of the early Church, decreed the baptism, though rendered in execrable Latin, to be valid because it was performed in good faith. Here as elsewhere, the spirit of truth rather than the observation of forms was for the Church the deciding factor. But an organization like the Church, depending for its unity and control on the general intelligibility of language, could not long endure a situation in which its priestly functionaries were effectively divorced from precise knowledge of its forms and instructions, as was this Bavarian priest. The European hierarchy was soon faced with a choice: either preserve Latin as the official language of bureaucracy and power and enforce its use according to universally accepted rules of usage or acquiesce in the reality of vernacular dialects. The first course would assure the Church of a sound and decorous language of power while separating it from the spoken languages of the faithful; the second course would reaffirm its commitment to the ideology of the Word, while permitting organizational chaos.

In the Carolingian renaissance of the eighth and ninth centuries the European hierarchy simply ratified the existing situation and begrudgingly accepted the reality of two distinct literacies, one of authority centered on writing and one of the masses centered on speech. The Carolingian reforms, sponsored by Charlemagne and his dynasty, attempted to purify Latin and restore it to its classical dignity. They aimed to ensure that throughout the West men in power—and this largely meant churchmen—would speak and write a common language of power. The reforms were for the most part successful, for Europe continued for hundreds of years to conduct official business in a formal Latin everywhere intelligible to the trained elites who controlled the bureaucracies. This formal, correct Latin literacy manifested itself primarily in writing or in oratory. Meanwhile, the leaders of Charlemagne's time had to concede that another kind of literacy demanded recognition. The decrees of the Council of Tours, held in 813—the year before the death of Charlemagne—reflect his wish that the homilies of the Church be translated "into the rustic roman language or into German, so that the whole world can more easily understand what is said." The Church kept for itself a formal Latin literacy of power and acknowledged the existence of a competing literacy in the lives of the faithful, expressed in the spoken vernacular of the masses. These two literacies lived, now in uneasy detente and now in open conflict, until the Renaissance.

In the Carolingian reforms, the Church tacitly adopted the literacy of the empire that its founders had denounced and defeated. Ironically, the revolutionary credo of the spoken word passed to popular elements not directly under the control of the Church. The language of the south—Pro-

vençal—became the common tongue of poetry, which now
spoke with the same rough vigor the early Christians had
relished as a chief virtue of common Latin or the Greek
koine. Increasingly, the vernacular languages also co-opted
the spiritual vigor of the Latin of the early Church, and by
the time of Dante in the fourteenth century, the popular language was the choice for a writer seriously committed to the
revolutionary doctrines of the fathers of the early Church.
For Dante and other champions of the popular languages,
the vernacular was not a departure from the tradition of the
Church, it was its essence. More and more, Latin was conceived in the same way early churchmen had seen the decorous language of the empire: as a sublime but distant vehicle
of written expression lacking the capacity for revelation inherent in the spoken word. Even Thomas Aquinas, the most
prolific writer among churchmen, implicitly acknowledges
the deficiencies of Latin and of writing in his superb thir-
teenth-century communion hymn:

> visus, gustus, tactus in te fallitur;
> sed solus auditus tote creditur.
> credo quicquid dixit dei filius,
> nihil veritatis verbo verius.

> Sight, taste, touch are deceived in regard to you;
> Only hearing can fully be believed.
> I believe whatever the son of God has said,
> There is nothing truer than the Word of truth.

The Christian revolution had succeeded in giving Europe
a new literacy in which the spoken word was the nearest approach to the divine, and in Aquinas' time, Europe had a
triumphant culture of speech. Liturgy and sermon, not the
written page, provided universal access to cultural truths.
Lecture and debate were the modes of higher education, and
not only because books were expensive. After all, the economics of literacy in the medieval period had been in part

determined by the prevailing ideology. One reason books were costly was that scribes were few; scribes were few because the Church regulated their numbers by monopolizing formal education and training only as many as it wished. Classical civilization had many more writers and many more manuscripts in circulation. Written texts could have been widely available in the Middle Ages, but the Church monopolized their manufacture and restricted their flow by controlling the education of writers. Thus the Church created the civilization of speech that it had originally desired, only to discover that it had lost faith in the validity of those beliefs about language that had shaped its culture. The society was rooted in speech, but the Church had gradually adopted another literacy of formal procedure and written texts.

By the time of Aquinas and the schoolmen, Latin had become a formal language used in official orations and texts and practiced according to certain well-established rules. Latin was so much the language of power that it became synonymous with writing and grammar. Dante could write in his *De vulgari eloquentia,* "Grammar is a kind of unchangeable identity of speech in different localities, times and places." By grammar he means Latin, and by Latin he means the official, written language of the European hierarchy. Dante's point about grammar, really a point about literacy, reflects the ideology of the European establishment throughout the medieval period. It is a literacy whose mechanical expression is writing and whose spirit is elitist, formal, rational, distant, and esoteric. Above all, it is a literacy—though adopted by the Church—curiously alien to the literacy of Christianity in its first centuries.

In John of Salisbury, that polymath of the twelfth century, the relation between grammar, Latin, and social power is made perfectly clear. "We find men," he writes in his *Metalogion,* "who profess all the arts, liberal and mechanical, but are ignorant of this very first one [grammar] without which it is futile to attempt to go on to the others. While other studies may also contribute to letters [*litteratura*, cultivation], grammar alone has the unique privilege of making one lettered [*litteratum*, literate]."

The nineteenth century resurrected John's definition of literacy. The literate man is the master not simply of a variety of mechanical skills necessary for reading and writing, but of grammar, which is the knowledge of how language works. In this view, the knowledge of grammar and language cannot be gained "in two, or even three years"; it is rather the object of lifelong education, and involves the study of philosophy and the acquisition of correct forms of expression. For John, grammar is man's free invention, but it imitates nature and in part grows out of it. In some sense it is what John calls it elsewhere, "a clean footprint of nature impressed on human reason." John was the Chomsky of his day: the knowledge of grammar gives access to the universal principles of reason, and reason is an imitation of the divine scheme of things. He who understands language and grammar knows God's plan.

John's views on grammar are generally those of the schoolmen of the Middle Ages. Later they would be Descartes' views as well. In each case their view of grammar is the product of a society that has come to rely on a fixed, written language governed by rules of correct expression. This attitude toward grammar is symptomatic of the literacy of the medieval establishment: language is no longer a vehicle of direct revelation, but, rightly understood, a blueprint of the natural plan. It is not itself truth, but a clue to truth. The literate man is not directly inspired by the truth of God's spoken Word. Instead he is studious of His purpose and tries to make it out in the books of nature and of language. God's Word is a text to be read, and the faculty of reading is a special skill with elite practitioners. Scholasticism's treatment of the Word is always mediated, never enthusiastic. The idea of correct writing permeates this attitude. A literacy of this sort is not accessible to the masses. It is the property of the *litterati*, those who understand reading, writing, interpretation, and correct forms of expression.

The combination of formal Latin and hierarchical organization, depending upon correct, written communication, went a long way toward facilitating the rationalistic approach to philosophy typical of the medieval thinker. More so perhaps than for Renaissance thinkers, his was an ideology of the book, even though the majority of the population could neither read nor write. What we call the Renaissance was a complex reaction to this literacy.

The movement of the late medieval and Renaissance periods toward the vernacular was in part a rebellion against the canons of fixed usages, of correct Latin, and of written authorities. All these had been objects of scorn to the early Christians, and the Christian ideology merely reasserted itself when the language of the Church became the thing it had previously rejected: a formal, official language standing between the faithful and the inspiration of the divine message, revealed in the spoken word.

The first Christian centuries present us with the spectacle of competing conceptions of literacy struggling with one another for dominance. If the knowledge of reading and writing waned throughout Europe, that was not simply the result of a general decline in the culture. The failure of reading and writing was balanced by the revolutionary literacy established by the Church, in which the mechanical skill of writing was restricted to an elite both for their benefit in wielding power and for the protection of the masses against the deformities of truth believed necessarily to be present in formal written languages. A society proceeding on such a revolutionary premise is not illiterate. It is rather operating from a doctrine that ascribes to language the highest degree of sanctity. God reveals himself to men in language. This revelation is clearest and most sublime in its primary form—speech. Other forms of language must be scrutinized with the most devout care to protect against the contamination of human error. Rhetoric and writing are especially suspect because these have traditionally been the means employed by the elites who opposed the early Church and because each is an art, a technology of the human intellect, and therefore capable of perverting the divine Logos. These technologies are best controlled by the Church itself, whose superior knowledge of their nature provides some check on their abuse. This extreme doctrine of Christian literacy held its own for the first five centuries after Constantine, but finally fell victim to the Church's need for a formal written language of its own.

By the late Middle Ages, formality and Latin were practically synonymous, and because most Latin was in writing, writing was also regarded as inherently formal. Writing became more and more the property of a special class trained in its arcana. The secrets of writing might be merely technical, as they were in the specialized vocabularies of the scholastics, or they might be overtly mystical, as they were for students of the Cabala or for St. Francis, who picked up any scrap of writing he found because, he is reported to have told a follower, "These letters are that from which the name of God is made up."

The forces of change at work in medieval Europe aimed in part to overthrow the correct Latin of the hierarchy and to rescue writing from the dreary eminence where it was revered as a mysterious tool of authority. Plato and Augustine would be models for those who sought reform because both had attempted a marriage between the inspired spontaneity of speech and the rational propriety of writing. The new men of the Renaissance wanted a return to a literacy in which speech was used with popular and creative intensity as a means of apprehending living truth. The literacy of the Church no longer provided such a model.

LITERACY AS BATTLEGROUND: THEN AND NOW

The history of literacy in the classical and medieval periods illustrates two general principles. First, literacy, no matter what kind, is used for power. Second, the relations of literacy and culture are always reciprocal.

In any society, men use literacy, however it has evolved, to further their own interests. In oral societies, those who have perfected the techniques of rhetoric—an Odysseus or a Chief Joseph—have an advantage over others, and the wise ruler is quick to employ the most adept users of the prevailing literacy in his cause, whether they be poets, scribes, or speech-writers. The use of language in the exercise of power is certainly not startling, nor a unique feature of literacy. When Lévi-Strauss announces that writing has always become a tool of authoritarian elites, he does no more than note the obvious fact that all human technologies and innovations are used to promote the interests of those who possess them.

If literacy is always used toward power, however, there is no fixed rule that will tell us what cultural effects follow any set of attitudes or technologies. It would be very pleasant if we could assert that the introduction of writing always leads to a scientific frame of mind, which it did not in the Roman Empire, or that oral cultures are incapable of conceptualizing, which is disproved by reading Homer. These easy generalizations, however, ought to be defeated by the reciprocal nature of all literate and cultural relations. An innovation in literacy, like writing, will always be colored by the existing attitudes toward language and the economic structure of the culture where it is introduced. The innovation will then begin to alter the attitudes and the economy, and these alterations will in turn produce new innovations, and so on, reciprocally, each step in the process being particular to its time and place in history. Thus the attitudes of the early Church toward language fundamentally colored the uses of reading and writing in the first Christian centuries and were in turn fundamentally changed by these technologies. The results of reciprocity can be very surprising. In the case of the Christian community, the initial attitude had been to champion the truth inherent in the spoken word in the midst of a civilization that had widespread and highly developed technologies of reading and writing but little appreciation of oral spontaneity or popular spirituality. Through growing reliance upon writing and correct usage, however, the Church emerged from the first Christian millennium with an attitude toward language almost diametrically opposed to that with which it began. By the time of the schoolmen, the Church was the promoter of an artificial language primarily accessible through reading and writing in a culture where these skills had become scarce, while the secular world now championed an ideology that venerated the spiritual virtue of the spoken word.

At the present the West faces a crisis not unlike that of the Middle Ages. We have produced two literacies, one of formal language as encoded in grammars and dictionaries, another of the living language found in daily intercourse and in popular art. To some degree every culture faces this split between formal and informal discourse, between the language of power and the language of the streets. But with us the split has assumed troubling dimensions. The best evidence of this is the anxiety expressed about literacy in a succession of books, articles, and popular commentaries.

The first Christian centuries have a lesson to tell us. The present crisis will not be solved by better schools, new textbooks, or sterner discipline. It is at heart a struggle between two ideologies. One of these, advocating a formal, correct grammar, is at the moment the ideology of established authority. This literacy becomes increasingly distant from the people controlled by it. The other ideology, the ideology represented by the informal, oral literacy we see growing up around us, is as yet undeveloped. It is at present a movement without a messiah, a doctrine that awaits its fourth gospel. When these come, the battle will be joined in earnest. The question of literacy in the modern world will come up again in a later chapter.

CHAPTER FOUR

When Media Collide:
Literacy and the Advent of Print

The introduction of printing into Europe, it is generally supposed, acted like a drug on Western culture. Suddenly the Bible was accessible to the masses; scientific ideas could circulate widely and rapidly; classical texts that before had been available in only a very few copies were now open to perusal by the whole intellectual community. McLuhan claims that the printed book "intensified perspective and the fixed point of view," and thereby altered the basic outlook of Western man and led to "nationalism, industrialism, mass markets, and universal literacy and education." Print, he says, is the technological catalyst of private enterprise, teaching men new methods of "repeatable precision" that lead to the great art works of the Renaissance on the one hand and to military and commercial conglomerates on the other. Print is the embodiment of the modern mind—so we are told. The exaltation of print that reaches almost religious enthusiasm in McLuhan began early. Bacon linked it with gunpowder and the mariner's compass as one of the three technological innovations that changed the world.

The frame of mind that is capable of forwarding these claims—on behalf of any medium—bedevils our culture, and compels us to look for precise causal connections where scientific accuracy is unlikely, in the often bizarre and always remarkable flux of civilization. There can be no doubt that printing, like television, radio, film, and the other new technologies of literacy developed in the last hundred years, contributed to reshaping Western culture, but those who assert that print somehow is the direct cause of a fundamental reformation of the European mind do a disservice to the very energies they seek to explain. A similar disservice is done today to television. In both cases, the argument runs something like this: a new technology is introduced. Soon the technology begins to act like a DNA molecule, encoding existing cells within the body of society with information that dictates new mental structures. The new medium alters the way people think, and these altered minds replicate the new mental structures from generation to generation. Many people now view television as a kind of virus, coopting the healthy brain cells of our young and permanently stamping them with a television mentality.

This perception of literacy and its technologies is both simple-minded and frightening. It asks us to believe that the operations of culture are mechanical, and that, once unleashed, the forces of technology are monstrous and ineluctable. I once met a concerned mother who, to repel the dreaded television virus, had not only banned the perverting tube from her home but had in fact never mentioned to her six-year-old son that such a thing existed. The belief that technologies act in a simple causal way upon the fabric of mentality and culture leads directly to hysteria of this kind, which is little different from medieval reactions to the plague. Like all victims of panic, ancient and modern, these hysterics have an appointment in Samarra.

In this chapter I make a reply to the hysteria that regards modern media as a threat to civilization, decency, and progress. The age of print provides the most dramatic example of

what happens to a society when it undergoes a basic rear-
rangement of its media. The Gutenberg era will illuminate
our own.

MEDIA USE IS ORGANIC

Neither print nor television necessarily leads to any particular social result. Different cultures have used the technologies of print and television differently because they start
from different notions and adaptations of literacy. If print
automatically led to industrialism and the spirit of private
enterprise, China would have had the European Renaissance
by 1000 A.D. But the Chinese, who were the first to discover
print, never used it as the West did. In part the Chinese use
of print was governed by the unwieldy nature of their written characters and by the absence in their technology of a
rapid means of duplicating type. A Western printer has only
the twenty-odd letters of the alphabet to deal with, and these
Gutenberg manufactured rapidly as movable type. The Chinese printer, on the other hand, had thousands of basic characters to master, not cast in reusable alloy, but carved on
wooden blocks. Printing a book with movable type in China
could take as long as copying a manuscript by hand did in
the West.

The difference between the effects of print in East and
West, however, is not merely the result of differently developed technologies, but of different literacies and ideologies.
Even today China finds its characters a more genuine and
congenial expression of its culture than the Western alphabet, and the unique Chinese evolution of literacy affected
their use of printing as well. Once they had printed a book,
for instance, the Chinese sharply restricted the number of
copies available, as against the Western practice, which has
been to find wider and wider audiences. Among us, print did

not create a capitalist economy; rather an already existing tendency toward such an economy influenced the book trade. Gutenberg began life as a goldsmith, and his bourgeois origins helped to shape his invention. In China, where different ideas about literacy and economics prevailed, books continued to be supplied in limited editions even when larger printings would have been profitable. Mao distributed the little red book according to Western practice, and its mass distribution was as much a departure from the Chinese tradition as the critique of Chinese classical thought it contained.

A quick look around the globe reveals the diverse ways in which the societies of the world use television or newspapers. The curiously different results of these uses should persuade even a hysteric that the technologies of literacy always have reciprocal relations with the existing literacy of a society, and the results they induce are always unique. Printing for us is both a cause and an effect of that particular historical event, the European Renaissance. It would be silly to maintain that, if we could now find another civilization without print and introduce Gutenberg's invention into its midst, in 100 years it would necessarily produce a Shakespeare and develop a mercantile economy.

European print literacy began well before Gutenberg. It was compounded of the continuing dialectic between the two competing literacies of eye and ear fostered by the Christian revolution, the economic upheaval of the late Middle Ages, an increasing reliance on written documents, the reform of the copyists' script, the competition between Latin and the vernacular tongues to be the language of record, and the native zeal—or lack of it—inherent in various European populations for certain problems of language. These—or elements like these—will always interact and combine with any new technology in the evolution of the literacy of a civilization.

"GET IT IN WRITING!":
MEDIEVAL WRITTEN CULTURE

The English development of literacy and print is well documented and probably the most interesting example to an English-speaking audience. The state of literacy in medieval England resembled that throughout Europe in most particulars. By Alfred the Great's account, ignorance of Latin—the language of the Church and the hierarchy—was the rule rather than the exception throughout Britain at the time of Alfred's educational reforms in the ninth century. The business of social organization was largely conducted through oral record and report—by sermon, by speech in council, by spoken agreement. Contracts were recorded by oral declaration, a practice that the Anglo-Saxons would regret after the Conquest when the Normans asked landholders for proof of tenancy. The native population spoke a language remote from the Latin of the Church, and the usual distinction between the formal, rational language of ideology and the spontaneous, idiosyncratic speech of the people applied, except that in tenth-century England even the clergy were inept in Latin, like our eighth-century Bavarian priest who botched the baptismal rite.

No two peoples have identical kinds of literacy, however, and the English brand was early marked by a zeal not only for the native language but for the intricacies of language itself. By Alfred's time vernacular Old English had produced a distinguished literature and a fairly sophisticated audience. Alfred's reforms were designed to provide English translations of those books "most necessary for all men to know" to a population many of whom "know how to read English," the remainder to be trained in it, so that "all youth of free men now in the English people having the means to apply themselves, should be committed to learning, while they have no strength for other employment, until they are able to read

English well." Alfred's statements imply that, while the English had little expertise with Latin, a native literacy built around the vernacular had already developed and included widespread ability in reading and writing English, a remarkable achievement in an age when the native tongue was still regared as rustic and uncouth by the Continental hierarchy. How far Alfred's reform succeeded is a matter of debate. The fact of such a plan, however, is proof of an existing devotion to literacy.

More remarkable than the early development of vernacular English literacy is its quality, which may be gauged not only by famous products like *Beowulf* and *The Dream of the Rood,* but also by the less well known riddles that Old English produced, probably as early as the eighth century:

> A foe deprived me of life, took away my bodily strength; afterwards wet me, dipped me in water, took me out again, set me in the sun where I quickly lost the hairs I had. Afterwards the hard edge of the knife cut me, with all impurities ground off; fingers folded me, and the bird's delight sprinkled me over with useful drops. . . . If the sons of men will use me they will be the safer and the more victorious, the bolder in heart and the blither in thought, the wiser in mind. . . . Ask what my name is, useful to me; my name is famous, of service to men, sacred in myself.

The riddle describes a book: how the parchment is made from the sheep-skin and then written on with the bird's quill. It shows a society—at a period when the rest of Europe was oppressed by an ideological dispute between oral Christian literacy and formal, respectable Latin literacy—with a highly developed vernacular, a secular scribal tradition, and an audience of readers. What is more, in its form the riddle reveals a spirit inquisitive about language. Words are to be searched for answers that are not immediately apparent. The mechanisms of language are not merely "useful," as the riddle has it, but provocative and stimulating. The *Times* crossword puzzle and the decoding of the Germans' Ultra secrets are in descent from this tradition of literacy.

The Norman conquest seriously disrupted the existing literacy of the native English tradition by reinforcing the authority of Latin, the official, formal language of the European hierarchy, and by introducing yet another language of power, Norman French. The story of how, through interaction, these various languages combined to form modern English is well known. Our English is the product of a society exposed to at least three different languages and notions of literacy.

The presence in any culture of two or more languages in actual use in the affairs of life must always be a shaping force of that culture's literacy. All of medieval Europe, using both vernacular and Latin, confronted the phenomenon of translation. Where there is only one language, the speakers are prone to confound it and their communal identity. In these single-language groups, the common tongue is regarded as a mysterious repository of wisdom that non-speakers cannot share. For the ancient Greeks, to speak Greek was the *sine qua non* of cultural identity. Those who did not were all alike *barbaroi*—barbarians whose lack of Greek marked them as culturally alien. In societies like this, culture and language function seamlessly. In time, they become identical: the culture is the language, the language is the culture.

The Middle Ages had no such easy identification between culture and language. The whole population was constantly reminded that no one language sufficed for the business of life or embodied the whole culture. Latin prevailed in the Church and in the official documents. Traders and businessmen used a pidgin Latin as the *lingua franca* of their transactions. The native languages were used in daily affairs and had literatures of their own. Provençal meanwhile was the common language of lyric poetry. Every important utterance or thought sooner or later required translation. The king of Scotland paid homage to his English overlord in an address spoken in French, but the official transcript of the occasion was recorded *litteraliter*, "literally," which meant in Latin.

At least at the levels of society where any sort of state or international business was transacted, the population must have been acutely aware of the problems posed by language. No one language incorporated the whole of medieval culture, and each language was constantly under the scrutiny that translation dictates, for the translator must always ask himself, "What does this word really imply?" "What language best captures the sense?" It is no exaggeration to say that every educated man of the Middle Ages was at least bilingual, and as time went on there were more and more educated men, so that a very large fraction of the whole population was familiar with two or more languages.

A civilization always in the process of translation is apt to be tolerant of strangers, sensitive to the nuances of language, and skeptical of any claims that a particular tongue is the special organ of universal truth. For men in such a civilization the great cultural ideas exist beyond any one language and take various forms in various dialects. So Aquinas argues that what makes holy writ eternal and universal is a sense that surpasses language altogether: "The author of Holy Scripture is God, in Whose power it is to signify His meaning, not by words only (as man also can do), but also by things themselves." Every cultivated medieval mind must have been to a degree skeptical about language as an exact revelation of any truth. The process of translation soon dispels the illusion that any language is comprehensive or precise.

The bilingual literacy of the late Middle Ages posed a troubling question to believers in the sanctity of the Word. A man who knows several languages will wonder, if the Word is a direct revelation of divinity, then in what language does it speak? A tradition extending from Isidore of Seville to Frederick the Great asserts that the Word manifests itself in Hebrew, the language of the Garden of Eden, but medieval men, exposed to the vagaries of bilingualism, were not entirely illuminated by this conviction. Bilingualism posed a linguistic problem that finally found its answer in the populist doctrines of the Reformation, which sought to preserve the primacy of the Word by exalting the vernacular to a unique position of authority.

In England, translation was even more obviously a fact of life than elsewhere, since at least three languages were in common use for the affairs of state, Church, and daily routine. The eclecticism of Chaucer, who was a prolific translator as well as poet, is only the most obvious result of such a bilingual society. Nor was the frame of mind engendered by translation reserved to an elite. The native population had a zeal for the puzzles of language that quickly adapted itself to the circumstances of the Conquest. A reading knowledge of Latin and French would have been extremely useful to anyone dealing in real estate or trade, and outside the agricultural communities, where one language would have sufficed for most men, bilingualism and a knowledge of reading were increasingly widespread from the twelfth century on. The best evidence of this is the gradual extension of the privilege known as benefit of clergy. When originally instituted, benefit of clergy exempted churchmen from the processes of civil law. Its protection extended to all those who could read from the Latin Bible, the thought apparently being that a knowledge of Latin marked a man as a member of the hierarchy, and most probably as a member of the clergy. By the time the privilege was abolished in the fifteenth century, however, a substantial portion of the male population qualified for benefit of clergy because they could read Latin, and *clericus* no longer denoted a churchman but a man who could read. This increase in bilingual readers, probably a greater increase in England than elsewhere in Europe, was in part the natural result of having to do business in different languages. The bilingual atmosphere of England after the Conquest made men acutely conscious of the problems presented by language, and not surprisingly the English Reformation, when it came, centered on questions involving the sanctity and authority of different tongues.

The medieval English appreciation of the uses of language soon created a market for men skilled in the literacy of the time. Anyone involved in law, in politics, or in business conducted by contract increasingly had need of several languages and written documents. In the fifteenth century, Margary Paston, herself a prolific writer of letters, complained that the family steward was unwilling to write out the daily accounts and asked her husband to fire him. By then writing had become a usual accomplishment for anyone holding a supervisory position. Earlier in the period, the Church had been able to control both the form and the flow of the official language of Europe, but the new literacy exhausted the Church's capacities. The Church had neither the inclination nor the ability to train as many scribes as were now required by society for the business of copying. A new profession—that of scrivener, or secular copyist—filled the gap. In time the scrivener became a money-lender as well. He performed two offices necessary for the foundation of modern Europe, and both contrary to the practice of the Church. He was a usurer, busy setting the foundations of a capitalist economy, and a scribe, whose business in copying broke the ecclesiastical monopoly on official literacy.

These two occupations were appropriately joined in one person. The scrivener represented the coming revolution in literacy. He had all the skills of language possessed by his clerical counterparts but was under no constraint of authority. Like Gutenberg, the scrivener's interests were those of the emerging middle classes. As early as the twelfth century

Walter Map, a proto-humanist, could complain that "the high-born of our country disdain letters or delay to apply their children to them, although to their children only is it rightly permitted to study the arts. . . . Slaves on the other hand (the which are called peasants) are eager to nourish their base-born and degenerate children in the arts unfitted to their station, not that they may rise from their rudeness, but that they may revel in riches." Knowledge of reading and writing was powerfully stimulated by the profit motive, and increasingly the hierarchy lost control of its dissemination. At the extremes of society reading and writing might have gone uncultivated—the farm laborer and the aristocrat often had no access to them or no need of them. As late as 1433, Nicholas of Cusa proposed that secretaries attend the conclave of imperial German electors because the electors themselves might not be able to write. Aristocrats could always hire readers or scribes and thus remain untainted by the mechanics of literacy, but the new middle classes saw the social advantages of learning these skills, and Walter Map rightly perceived that the spread of the literate arts was a threat to the ruling classes.

As Walter Map saw, the Middle Ages was developing a kind of literacy that might be revolutionary in its application. The new literacy of written record, and later of print, had many apparent advantages, especially for the upwardly ambitious. Our bourgeois economy, evolved from the social forces at work in the late Middle Ages, still enjoys these advantages. They may be summed up in the phrase "surety of obligation." The obligation of the citizen is to follow "the letter" of the law, of the private individual, to honor his contracts. Men of the medieval era learned slowly the full benefit of written record. Some of their early contracts, for instance, often omit the date of the agreement, thereby giving much leeway for contention, but the principle behind the written record they fully appreciated. M. T. Clanchy estimates that the number of letters generated by the Papacy, by the French and by the English courts, increased by a factor of between four and six from 1100 to 1200. Increase in population or workload alone cannot explain such a dramatic rise in the use of written record. Europe had suddenly understood the grand idea that lies behind the cry "Get it in writing!" Written record furthers social order by fixing obligations beyond the uncertainty of speech or memory. When print appeared, it naturally exacerbated the record-keeping mania of the West, but the mania preceded the printing press and is intimately connected with the rise of a new capitalist economy and with the rise of nationalism. A secure system of obligations is at the heart of capitalism; a fixed set of civil and criminal codes surely enforceable is the soul of the national state.

Not that Europe greeted the age of written record with unalloyed enthusiasm. The spread of writing was not only a threat to the monopoly on official literacy enjoyed by the hierarchy. There is also something sinister about an obligation in writing. The pang of hesitancy most of us experience on signing a written commitment is only the most obvious manifestation of what we might call the Mephistophelean facet of written record. Mephistophelean because the archetypal image of the danger of written obligations is Faust's contract with the devil. The Faust legend was first published in 1587, but the contract signed in blood is an emblem that grows out of the Middle Ages. God, said Saint Paul, had made his people "ministers of the new testament; not of the letter, but of the spirit: for the letter killeth, but the spirit giveth life." The apostle's admonition conforms to the early Christian distrust of the formal, written language of empire; his suspicion reemerges in the Faust story, which in the incident of the contract is a natural reaction to the apparatus of written record founded in the medieval period. Written obligations mortgage the future, and therefore the aspirations, of mankind. Anyone who is in debt to his credit card knows as much. In Faust's case, the obligation murders the soul. Goethe's Faust denounces Mephistopheles for insisting upon the written agreement:

> Cannot you pedant do without a screed?
>
> . . .
>
> What, is it not enough my spoken word should force
> My days into eternal peonage?
> Does not the world rush on with brimming course,
> And I am to be prisoned by a pledge?

By fixing a present obligation as an unalterable future pledge, written record does what Lycurgus feared: for the sake of present comfort it stifles the creative capacity to reinterpret the past.

There is in written record a spirit of contention that has come to mark our civilization. The repossessed car and the repossessed soul are both emblematic of the operation of written obligations. As we have noted, the rise of capitalism depends upon agreements in writing, as does the practice of usury. It was no accident the scrivener should have doubled as a money-lender. When Shylock demands the satisfaction of his bond, he should be pictured brandishing the contract in one hand. In literature at least the very advantages of written record have been seen as unchristian and diabolical. Not only in literature, I think. There is a decidedly Mephistophelean cast to the whole age of written record.

THE WORD, THE PRESS, AND THE REFORMATION: JOHN WYCLIFFE

England and Europe had developed the new literacy of written record well before the advent of print. Print did not suddenly burst upon the European scene in the fifteenth century and transform an otherwise oral culture. The introduction of paper-making and Gutenberg's refinements provided the technical means for print, but the population of England, at least, was ripe for the invention. Northern Italy and the Netherlands also had extensively developed new styles of literacy at the dawn of the print age; not surprisingly, they became publishing centers. The spread of reading and writing skills had created a market for books, and the economic systems of the late Middle Ages predisposed industrious businessmen like Caxton and Gutenberg to fill a need where they saw one. Since the thirteenth century the public had grown accustomed to written records in business. The demand for texts had already risen sharply in the 200 years before Gutenberg. Print naturally met it.

Print, at least in the European example, was not a break with the past but the technological climax of a change in the literacy of the culture that had long been under way. Claims that print revolutionized European society, altered the nature of memory, reorganized perspective, and rang the death knell of oral culture must be examined with great care. Similar claims advanced on behalf of the new technologies of the modern age such as radio, cinema, and television, should be met with equal restraint.

A good case can be made that print was not revolutionary at all, but reactionary in its effects. The genuinely revolutionary struggle had been between the spoken vernacular languages and formal, written authority of Latin. Behind this opposition stood two conflicting types of literacy: the vernacular tradition claiming the immanence of the God in the Word, and the formal tradition arguing that language was but a reflection of the divine that required authoritarian interpretation. The advent of print at first greatly strengthened the Latinists, for the majority of books printed were classical texts and translations aimed at a learned audience. Because of its inborn need for uniformity on the page, printing itself intensified the need of formal Latin literacy for doctrines of correctness and fixed modes of usage. Besides his famous Bible, one of Gutenberg's first publications was Donatus' Latin grammar, the archetypal rule book of the formal literacy of the day. Even Caxton, who zealously produced the works of Chaucer and other authors of the English vernacular tradition, proclaimed again and again that he hoped printing would speed the process by which the native language acquired the same dignity and formality that Latin had formerly possessed. He made his books, he said in the preface to his translation of the *Aeneid*, "not for every rude and uncunning man to see, but to clerks and very gentlemen that understand gentleness and science"—that is, men educated in the correct forms and modes of interpretation, the very concepts against which the early Church, with its oral literacy, had railed when it praised the "rude and unlettered" believer.

The tradition of the rude believer, however, maintained its vitality through the Middle Ages and into the age of print. Governments realized early that it was not books, handwritten or printed, that caused trouble; it was their dissemination among a wide audience not trained in the correct modes of interpretation and the prevailing forms of authoritarian literacy. The Lollards, English dissidents of the fourteenth century whose heresies anticipate elements of Protestant theology, were condemned by the state because "they make and write books, they do wickedly instruct and inform the people." The Lollard error had been not simply to expound unorthodox theories, but to expound them to the masses, some of whom, because of the general spread of reading and writing skills, could have read their work, written not in Latin but in the native language.

The Lollards translated the Bible into plain English, a project the government condemned. The Lollard theory of literacy maintains that the living Word speaks directly to the faithful in their own tongue; that truth inheres in language; and that every man must be the interpreter of the divine message, communicated directly to him in Scripture—and usually heard, not read. "The Holy Ghost gave to the Apostles wit on Whit Sunday for to know all manner of languages to teach the people God's law thereby," wrote John Wycliffe, the English priest and teacher whose writing is the intellectual heart of fourteenth-century religious dissent. "And God would that the people were taught God's law in divers tongues." Behind Wycliffe's heresy lies a revolutionary theory that lends ideological backbone to the emerging bourgeois literacy of the late Middle Ages. In this theory there is a basic structure of truth inherent in all languages. This basic structure of truth is accessible to all human minds without any other assistance but their own wits. The Bible, directly inspired by God as Word, is the one sure and unsullied manifestation of truth in language. In it, language is not a barrier to understanding or to action. It *is* understanding and action. The connection of such an ideology with the growth of individualism and with empiricism is clear. Descartes's *cogito*, the assertion that the unaided mind operating purely on the basis of its own experience may find the essence of truth in language, is only the most obvious fruit of this literacy. In our own day, Chomsky has repeated this heresy in the form of a linguistic rather than a religious argument, and he rightly calls his heresy Cartesian, for the metaphysics of Descartes rests upon similar premises.

The literacy inspired by this view was one that glorified language. It cast its lot with the vernacular and asserted that a man may find in his own language and experience the elements of eternal verity. This new literacy was a direct challenge to existing authority. When each man is his own interpreter of language, hierarchies are doomed. In England as elsewhere the ruling classes found in formal, written language, whether Latin or Norman French, a mighty tool of social order, but not an indispensable one. It could not, however, do without authoritative interpretation. Authoritative interpretation is dependent on the brand of literacy that had held sway in Europe since the Carolingian reforms and the first scholastics. It encompasses the view that language is a complex medium that lowers a veil between truth and the human mind. This veil is penetrated only by rhetorical and interpretive skills that require much training and discipline. In this formal system, language can only express truth when exercised with the most careful attention and studied restraint. Against this literacy, Wycliffe asserted that "the Bible had its own grammar or logic, which could be grasped, literally and mystically, by understanding it as God conceived it," in the words of Gordon Leff's study of medieval heresy. In later Protestant developments of Christianity, Wycliffe's thought becomes central. "At bottom," said Adolf Harnack, the great Lutheran theologian, Luther reduced all the sacraments of the Church "to one only, namely, the Word of God," fully revealed in Christ's preaching and accessible in its wholeness and simplicity to the faithful. Truth is immanent in language; the Bible is language perfected; every man can receive this truth without mediation, using the powers inborn in mind and spirit.

The development of this new literacy preceded the age of print and is in many respects not even dependent upon the growth of written record, for it looks back to the oral tradition of the early Church and to the venerable Christian heritage of opposition to formal or hierarchical systems of interpretation. The Lollard stress on preaching confirms the movement's ties to the oral foundations of Christianity and presents us with a paradox: here was a movement that anticipates Protestantism, the individualistic ethos, and the mass dissemination of reading and writing skills, yet in its operations it is reactionary and oral. The solution to the paradox is eloquent witness to the way in which conflicting cultural elements were synthesized in the age of written record and print.

Lollardy looked backward to the age of the Gospels, not forward to the age of technology. Yet the logic of the Lollard position argued for the universal availability of texts, and this logic, coupled with the growing medieval ability to produce written texts and later with the advent of print, facilitated the rise of reading and writing skills. With these skills came the new kinds of social structure, like bureaucracy and business, that go with increased mechanical capacity in reading and writing. The connection between Protestant fundamentalism and the rise of modern economic systems is in part ironic: by seeking to reestablish early Christian literacy the fundamentalists offered a philosophy that, in conjunction with new technologies, has led to the mass secular literacy of the modern era. Just as curiously, the authoritarian school of interpretation that Wycliffe and his spiritual descendents opposed did not resist the advent of print or of more widely disseminated texts. Far from it. The schoolmen had after all created both the motive and the opportunity for more copyists by establishing an elite but growing group of interpreters each in need of texts. The members of this growing elite were the first to utilize print as a means of disseminating authoritative texts throughout their ranks.

The state did not oppose writing any more than it later opposed print. It did, however, vigorously oppose the notion that what was written or printed was subject to any but disciplined, formal, and authoritative analysis. To protect its established literacy, Church and state combined in Wycliffe's time to license not writing but preaching. Writing itself, and printing afterwards, were not threats so long as what was written or printed was read in an orthodox way, but Wycliffe taught a new style of reading that challenged the right of the hierarchy to control interpretation. The establishment sought to restrict not the flow of writing but the spread of primitive Christian literacy as rediscovered by Wycliffe and the first Protestants after him. Used according to its literacy, the hierarchy had no quarrel with writing or printing. Used according to Wycliffe's theories, however, writing and then printing became subversive media that threatened the power of the Church and the state.

The doctrine of the living Word was potentially as dangerous to Renaissance England as it had been to imperial Rome, and the English government took the necessary measures to combat it. By prohibiting a vernacular Bible it assured that an authority would have to stand between the book and the believer in order to interpret the book for him. By opposing the domination of Rome the government guaranteed that this authority would be under the jurisdiction of the English crown, not the Papal court. Once the Tudor reforms had made sure of the loyalty of the clergy by bringing them under the control of the state, then an English Bible was permitted because the interpreters were secure. But the role of technology in this period, or in our own for that matter, is by no means as straightforward as the religious and philosophical conflicts in which it was employed by both sides as a weapon. To understand the conflicts and the role of print, we must look at two Englishmen from opposed camps and examine their relation to the word and to its technologies.

THE TEXT, THE PRESS, AND ORTHODOXY: JOHN DONNE

John Donne is perhaps the foremost champion of secure interpretation in the English Renaissance. Donne's career as poet, priest, scholar, and humanist illustrates the central themes of his period and provides an excellent example of the ways in which the growth of written record and the advent of print influenced orthodox ideology in the period encompassed by his dates, 1571-1631. Donne's work is everywhere indebted to print. Like Robert Burton, the author of

The Anatomy of Melancholy, his universal learning was only possible when classical texts were widely available, a phenomenon made possible first by the increase in manuscript copies and later by Gutenberg's invention. But Donne's work, for all that its range and polish are the products of print, is still largely oral in form and authoritarian in purpose. Its breadth was revolutionary, but its tone was consonant with the medieval period. When in one of his sermons Donne issues a caution about laymen reading Scripture in the vernacular, he epitomizes the stance of the European hierarchy at the Renaissance. There is nothing surprising in this. Donne was born into a Catholic family. He aspired to position in the Protestant government of the day. Both by birth and by inclination he belonged to a tradition that supported authority. His views on language, faith, and the Bible reflect this predisposition. Scripture for Donne is the chief means of our knowledge of God, "but the Scripture in the Church." "First learn at church and then meditate at home; receive the seed by hearing the Scripture interpreted here, and water it by returning to those places at home." As a priest in the Church of England, Donne, like Aquinas and the Catholic clergy of the Middle Ages, insists that what is divine in language is also problematical and known surely by the trained exegete only. The general availability of texts was to him no substitute for the imposition by authority of correct interpretation. For Donne, the masses were still to get this interpretation by ear: "receive the seed by hearing the Scripture interpreted here." So far, at least, Donne would have been at home in the thirteenth century.

Behind Donne's position is a kind of literacy informed by the arts of print but rooted in the medieval literacy of the Latin Church:

> My God, my God, Thou art a direct God, may I not say a literall God, a God that wouldest bee understood literally, and according to the plaine sense of all that thou saiest?

But thou art also (Lord I intend it to thy glory, and let no
prophane misinterpreter abuse it to thy diminution) thou
art a figurative, a metaphoricall God too; A God in whose
words there is such a height of figures, such voyages, such
peregrinations to fetch remote and precious metaphors,
such extentions, such spreadings, such Curtaines of Alle-
gories, such third Heavens of Hyperboles, so harmonious
eloquutions, so retired and so reserved expressions, so
commanding perswasions, so perswading commandments,
such sinewes even in thy milke, and such things in
thy words, as all prophane Authors, seeme of the seed
of the Serpent, that creepes, thou art the Dove, that flies.
O, what words but thine, can expresse the inexpressible
texture, and composition of thy word; in which, to one
man, that argument that binds his faith to beleeve that to
bee the Word of God, is the reverent simplicity of the
Word, and to another, the majesty of the Word, and in
which two men, equally pious, may meet, and one wonder,
that all should not understand it, and the other, as much,
that any man should.

In this view of God, language is never a spontaneous or obvious revelation of his truth, but like Nature itself, a complex,
corruptible product of the divine hand. The human mind
cannot instantly intuit truth in language, but must instead
arrive at it by a process of discipline and study. It follows
that written or printed texts, whether Scripture or the odes
of Horace, cannot speak directly to the untrained reader. Authority must keep a check on the multiplication of texts. It
has a special responsibility to regulate all interpretation, and
the pulpit is the first line of defense against the spread of un-
informed reading. Donne hardly ever quotes Scripture in his
sermons without providing the Latin of the Vulgate, his own
translation, and then his interpretation—a procedure emblematic of the literacy of the European hierarchy at the Renaissance: control the text, control its translation, control its
interpretation.

Humanists like Donne did not so much displace as co-opt

the authority of the medieval schoolmen. Like the enemies of Wycliffe, they were devoted to the text, to its privileged interpretation, and to its limited availability. The restricted and priestly nature of their literacy is clearly seen in the Italian humanists, so many of whom, like Ficino and Pico della Mirandola, harked back to magical, and therefore exclusive, systems of interpretation like astrology or the Cabala.

THE WORD AND REVOLUTION:
JOHN BUNYAN

But another type of literacy, a type descended from Wycliffe, flourished side by side with Donne's. Its postulates are most clearly stated in the works of the dissenting Protestant John Bunyan, whose simple writing style, compared with Donne's ornate periods, reflects both a different faith and a different literacy. Donne spent his life inside the established Church and gloried in the heritage of scholasticism. Bunyan began life as a village tinsmith, served from 1644 to 1646 as a common soldier in the Parliamentary army, and became a preacher in the nonconforming Protestantism that in the English Revolution challenged and temporarily abolished the established order to which Donne belonged. Bunyan looked not to the Fathers of the Church for his faith but to the plain language of the Gospels. In his spiritual autobiography, *Grace Abounding to the Chief of Sinners*, Bunyan explains the emotional and ideological fervor he felt when he read the Bible. His religious zeal hinges on a revolutionary new type of literacy: "Now also I should labour to take the Word as God had laid it down, without restraining the natural force of one syllable thereof." Here language is pure emanation from God. It has a clear and natural purpose intelligible to anyone possessed of soul—that is, to any mortal, trained or not in interpretation. Language is not a mysterious barrier between mind and truth, it is truth itself. Every man has "a right to the Word," and the Word studied in faith always yields truth. Faith, accessible to all, is the means to wisdom.

Wycliffe's and Bunyan's theories of the Word naturally generated a literacy likely to promote the wide dissemination of texts and the ability to read them, and Protestantism has rightly been linked with the spread of reading and writing skills in Northern Europe and America. But several caveats are in order. Donne's kind of literacy made more *use* of texts than Bunyan's, since in it language is regarded as a puzzle behind which the divine is hiding. For Donne and his school, books must be read and reread, each sentence approached with every resource the soul and mind can muster in order to make it yield up its truth. Donne's own poetry provides a test for this method. Written or printed record is part of this literacy as much as it is of Bunyan's, but in a different way.

In Bunyan's kind of literacy, on the other hand, language is not so much an object of study as a point of departure for the enraptured soul. For Bunyan, language itself, properly used (and proper use depends not on training but on faith), has few complexities. Its sense is transparent and each man is endowed with the means of correct interpretation if only he will use it. The goal of this literacy is not to instruct the mind in the complexities of language but to train the soul in the purity of faith that reveals language in its essential simplicity. One is a literacy of the mind descended from the Middle Ages; the other is a literacy of the soul descended from the enthusiasts of the early Church. One form of literacy preserved the written text for elucidation by the hierophants, the other disseminated it for the enlightenment of the masses.

In both systems the oral tradition continued to play a central part. For Donne, the preacher is an essential link in the chain of authority. He bridges the gap between those who read and know and those who hear and are instructed. For Bunyan, speech is the medium of divine revelation, and a man who has in simplicity of heart understood Scripture is called upon to profess his faith in words. But in Bunyan's literacy, language is synonymous with action, while in Donne's it is the very opposite of action. For Donne, action lies beyond language, and good action is only possible where the tricks and nuances of language have been exhausted. Hamlet's "The rest is silence" echoes this view. Donne's writing mimics the attitude. In his sermons or in his lyrics, language leads to deeds, whether the deed be holy dying or witty seduction, but the deeds themselves are beyond language. His approach is that no true or just action can proceed until the linguistic impediment between man and meaning has been dismantled.

Bunyan, on the other hand, considered language, when used by the faithful, to be pure, and speech to be equivalent to action. Hence the conjunction in Cromwell of plain-spoken words and deeds. Cromwell, the archetypal new man in seventeenth-century politics, is also a good example of the new literacy in action. His epigrammatic utterances were for him and his followers a sanctified form of activity. "You are no Parliament, I say you are no Parliament," he said as he prorogued the remnant of the Long Parliament. His concise statement is now called by linguists performative utterance because the very act of speaking accomplished the thing spoken of. The performative utterance may stand as the type of the new literacy of Wycliffe, Bunyan, and Cromwell. In it, speech is truth in action.

THE MILTONIC COMPROMISE: OLD MADE NEW

The two literacies represented by Donne and Bunyan are rarely found in such uncontaminated splendor. I have used them as examples because they give the essence of two opposed positions not usually encountered in their pure form.

They are often found in combination—brilliantly so in the case of Milton. As the son of a scrivener, Milton was born to the new Protestant literacy. His family's prosperity was the result of the age of written record and the capitalist economics that accompanied it. Not surprisingly, his religious sympathies inclined to the Lollard position, now more fully elaborated by radical Protestants of the same school Bunyan would later represent. But Bunyan's literacy was clearly reflected in his style, which is limpid and direct, forceful and sincere. Milton's language, on the other hand, is grand and baroque. It hardly seems to be vernacular at all. It is sinuous, allusive, and complex. Readers may feel that the language of Milton's poetry and prose is no incarnation of the living Word, but an imposing barrier between truth and understanding, a barrier that must, in the tradition of Donne and the medieval hierarchy, be torn down by patient and informed interpretation.

Milton, I think, reconciled the two opposed literacies of his time by taking from the one its formality, its classicism, and its elitist attitude and by subjecting these elements to the psychological method implied in the other, the revolutionary literacy of Wycliffe and Bunyan. Milton meant to reinterpret the texts of the old literacy not by authority but by the disciplined soul. Milton thus embraces the two competing literacies of his time, and this is essential to his greatness. Like Wycliffe and Bunyan he meant his reader to have a direct, unmediated experience in reading the text, but he saw the text as necessarily dense with authority and tradition. For Donne authority and tradition demanded trained exegetes; for Milton they demanded trained readers who could experience the weight and complexity of what they read with the same spontaneity and spiritual intensity Wycliffe or Bunyan expected from the believer who heard or read the illuminating Word of God in his native language. Thus Milton devoted much of his attention to educational reforms that would make each man not merely a reader but an exegete as well. Milton demanded more than simple faith and mechanical skill in reading from his audience; he demanded an educated reader, but one who nevertheless experiences his poetry as personal revelation.

With men like Donne, Bunyan, and Milton the old debate between the two literacies of Europe continued. But the men of the English Renaissance were not replicas of their ideological counterparts in earlier centuries. Donne is not a copy of Aquinas nor Bunyan of Wycliffe. The difference—what makes these men at once partisans in an enduring debate and yet marks them as inhabitants of their own time—is in part due to printing. Printing exacerbated the traditional conflict between the literacies of the Word and the text. It also assured that the debate would continue in the context of modern technology. For both parties, print and its technology became an essential element of literacy—for the authoritarians as a means of preserving texts and educating the elite, for the popular party as a means of spreading the truth inherent in language used by faith.

Print grounded the old questions about literacy in the technological revolution that transformed the West. Print grew directly out of the same set of scientific and economic facts that have made the modern West, and despite its role as a catalyst for ideas, it is not so much a cause as a part of that development.

Hence Bacon's conviction that printing is one of the three innovations that changed the world. As the texts and ideas of the Western tradition gradually emerged in print, they were rejuvenated—perhaps even reincarnated. By way of elucidation, we might point to Billy Graham or Jerry Falwell and note that the message they preach is almost 2000 years old. It is the same message preached by Paul to the Galatians or Livingstone to the Matabele. Yet because Graham and Falwell preach on television, the message is somehow changed.

It is too much to say that the medium is the message, but certainly the medium colors the message. The same food stored in metal or plastic acquires a distinct flavor from its container. So print gave its flavor to the old debate over literacy. Like the television preacher, it made the old seem new, by inviting men to consider once again the traditional issues arranged in neat rows of type of uniform style. The conjunction of the old debate and the new technology did not, I think, favor any one position. Instead it made the whole issue seem pertinent, much as the Christian ministry of the airwaves compels even the cynic once again to confront the traditional issues of Christian dogmatics.

Print was a part of the new science. Its practitioners were not churchmen but laymen. It was a profit-making enterprise. The flavor of print was capitalistic, bourgeois, and progressive, and since the age of Gutenberg and Caxton, literacy in the West has assimilated this flavor, about which Chapter Five will have more to say. But if print lent its flavor to English thought at the start of the modern period, it did not create an instant revolution, either technological or psychological. The Church had made Europe a culture of the ear more than the eye, and the old orientation died hard, if it died at all.

Print by its nature is easily subject to control, while the spoken word is not. Governments may seize presses, destroy type, tax paper, and censor books—all with relative success. They are hard pressed, however, to suppress talk except by the most extreme measures. Nor did governments need to regulate print very closely in its early days, for print had close ties with the language of power and the doctrine of correctness. The danger of print was that it was introduced into a society where the elite consumers of books had before its advent already been exposed to an alternative theory of reading. The Lollard approach to holy writ, which extremists like Milton extended to all authoritative texts, assumes that without interpretation or guidance each reader can intuit the meaning of what he reads. Reading thus becomes revelation—a doctrine abhorrent to Church and state alike because it destroys the rationale for hierarchy. This new approach was the harder to resist because it paradoxically asserted its own authority in the same Christian tradition its detractors claimed to be defending.

Print facilitated the spread of this new approach by gradually extending the number of elite readers and by providing them the authoritative texts upon which their challenge to authority rested. Curiously, the threat print posed to authority was not that the masses would become voracious readers of incendiary tracts but that the authorities and exegetes from whom they habitually took their opinions would themselves become infected with new ideas. The notion that one ought to listen to no other authority but the indwelling Word was itself propounded by men who were believed because they spoke with great authority, men who for the most part made their points in speech, not print. The message of Cromwell's speeches may have been liberty of the individual conscience, but it was a lesson the listeners accepted largely in the spirit of deference to the speaker's authority.

A student of literacy must be careful to take into account not only the number of readers and writers in a society, but also the number who are indirectly influenced by the spoken word of readers and writers. The influence may be very direct, as when one reader reads to a group of non-readers, or it may be more subtle, as when a Cromwell, himself changed by what he has read, in turn persuades a large following, not by writing, but by rhetoric and the inspiration of the spoken word. Print was revolutionary not because it replaced authority or rhetoric but because it helped to alter their basic nature, and this alteration had already begun when print was introduced.

The government in England assured that texts would not

be widely available for general reading by limiting the number of presses in operation and the number of books permitted in each printing. In Elizabethan England, only 1200 or 1500 copies of any book were allowed to be printed from one setting of type. Print was not immediately a tool of mass enlightenment. It was rather the oral tradition, perpetuated by educated men who no longer subscribed to the established literacy and who appealed to mass audiences in their native language, that then threatened the established order. The renegade priest was subject to the most severe penalties— even death for heresy. The renegade bookseller rarely risked more than a fine. Church and government recognized that the danger of print was not a huge reading public but a growing and vocal intellectual community straining at the bonds of traditional authority and eager to spread the Word.

PRINT AND TELEVISION

One thing is certain: the growth of a reading public and the advent of print did not instantly transform the European mind. Today many people fear the advent of the television brain, which is supposed to be purely oral and visual, cool, detached, and prone to violence when not engaged in its favorite activity, vegetation. Owners of television minds alternate between states of sexual excitement and narcolepsy. They are routinely manipulated by sinister forces only slightly less mindless than themselves whose object is to strip them of money and dignity while poisoning them with sugar, fluorocarbons, and tawdry dogmas. Anyone exposed to television for protracted periods of time is almost certain to develop narcissism, acne, and fascist tendencies. On the other hand, the age of print is supposed to have created a mass audience that was disciplined, studious, and vigorous in the championship of humane ideals. After Gutenberg, Europeans adopted a scientific and realistic attitude toward life, learned self-reliance, and gained perspective, all from the suddenly acquired habit of looking at neatly justified pages of print.

As we have seen, nothing of the sort happened. Print is first an effect, and later a cause, in European history. If it changed the European mind, it did so very gradually. Before Gutenberg, many men, and growing numbers of them, could read in at least one language, yet the society in which they lived was still highly oral. Reading and writing had not driven out rhetoric and sermons, nor would they ever.

There is no good evidence besides modern wishful thinking that the increase in written record and the advent of printed texts immediately altered the capacities or functions of human memory. Instead, print was part of a chain of events associated with the natural evolution of European literacy. After it appeared, it existed in combination with forms of oral culture, many of which, like the sermon or the drama, were not driven out by the printing press and the spread of reading ability, but supplemented and invigorated by the contact. The plays of Shakespeare or the sermons of Donne are certainly informed by a wider variety of texts and ideas than might have been possible before Gutenberg, but they were meant to be heard for all that. The appearance of an English Bible did not thwart, it stimulated memorization of the sacred text, and print culture alone cannot explain the emergence of rational and linear views of history and science. Peter Abelard and William of Occam had the rational spirit without benefit of print.

The lesson that the coming of print teaches is of some comfort to our century. New technologies do not drive out old forms of literacy. Rather, the new technology, be it print or television, lives side by side with the existing state of literacy and gradually blends with it in complex ways that change but do not necessarily diminish or abolish it. Print and written record did not destroy but supplemented the oral literacy in which they emerged. The new electronic media will not destroy print and written record. Men did not stop speaking, preaching, or doing these well because of print. They will not stop reading, writing, or doing these well because of television. If they did, the fault would not be electronic. It would be because we have a shabby notion of language.

Or no notion of it. The saddest case an English teacher encounters is the student who cannot write at all. This student does not write enough to have grammatical problems. His essays are rarely more than fifty words long. At the end of his final exam he writes, "Sorry, I can't think of anything else." The first time I encountered one of these airheads I assumed he was the victim of electronic media. I asked about his reading and viewing habits. "Do you read books or magazines?" "No." "I guess you watch a lot of tv." "No." "You must watch a little?" "We don't own a tv." "Movies?" "I never go to movies." The student was isolated from almost all media, newspapers, radio, records, everything. "What do you do?" "Well, mostly I feed my rabbit."

The electronic media will give us a new kind of literacy, but consider the alternative: a nation of rabbit-feeders. Even if it were possible to stifle the spread of television viewing, the age of print would not return. A 1980 study of teenage television viewing and reading habits by Michael Morgan in the *Journal of Communication* gives some hard evidence for the conclusion toward which this chapter points. According to Morgan's figures, teenagers "who are heavy viewers early on are the ones who read more later." Morgan suggests that "during later adolescence students tend to be heavy or light users of *both* media at the same time. For many, then, consistent light viewing may be symptomatic of lack of involvement with media in general." In the Renaissance, oral, written, and print media competed for dominance. Each influenced the others, and each became a means of ideological expression. The best minds of the Renaissance did not choose one medium over another but used them all. The best minds of the next generations will draw on print and television. Theirs will be a new literacy influenced by all available media, not relying on one alone. It will be a different literacy, not a worse literacy than our own. The alternative to television is not a return to the age of print but dead air in the mind.

What the present age of electronic media needs is fewer Jeremiahs and more Miltons. Milton united the classical literacy of the medieval Church with the revolutionary literacy of the Protestant Reformation. In our own day we will have to learn to master the methods and styles of the old print literacy and adapt them to the creative impulse of the new electronic media. In any event, our present approach is untenable. An official literacy, closely allied with print, tries desperately to maintain its authority in the face of a new literacy tied to electronics. The old literacy devotes much energy to denouncing the new, the new literacy studiously ignores the old. Until some Miltonic wedding can be made between these two camps, we will continue to live in a world of divisive literacies.

CHAPTER FIVE

Iran to Ann Landers: Fallacies about Literacy and Development

Literacy is a complex cultural phenomenon involving relations between attitudes toward language and mechanical skills. No statistics will ever adequately describe the often curious and always intricate ways in which various civilizations have treated language, and there will always be a privileged place in the study of literacy for the philologist and the philosopher as well as the social scientist. The job of assessing literacy, however, is considerably easier where reliable data are available about its mechanical manifestations—reading, writing, print, and its other technologies. In our century we have if anything too much information of this sort, but the past presents a motley collection of conflicting data leading to no certain conclusions. Historians cannot agree on the population of ancient Athens or Rome, much less on the number of readers or writers they contained. England, the country whose rates of reading and writing have been most thoroughly explored, also presents a dim picture before the nineteenth century. One source from the fifteenth century announces that, of twenty pilgrims, fewer than three could be expected to repeat one of the ten commandments or say the pater noster, while studies of the merchants of medieval

London at this same time indicate that some 50 percent could read English. In 1533 Sir Thomas More asserted that more than 40 percent of the kingdom had not yet learned to read English, implying that over half could. Twelve years later, the bishop of Winchester claimed that "not the hundreth part of the realm" could read.

Similar confusing statistics could be adduced for each period of history up to our own. They provoke two questions. First, how can we make sense out of them, and second, but more important, why should we bother to do so?

The necessity of studying the number of readers and writers grows out of the use to which such figures have already been put by social historians and scientists, who have for some years been examining the relation between literacy and different kinds of social development—economic, psychological, and cultural. The results of these examinations shape the policy of developing nations, of educational curricula here and abroad, and of social planners everywhere. We are obliged, if only as a matter of self-defense, to look at these figures with the greatest care. This chapter examines the claims made by social scientists for literacy as a tool of economic and mental development.

SKILL IN READING AND WRITING DOES NOT A MIGHTY NATION MAKE

The statistician of literacy faces two preliminary problems: defining what he means by literacy and deciding what evidence he will use to prove its presence or absence. Both of these endeavors have proven difficult.

Literacy is generally defined in one of three ways: as the simple ability to read, and sometimes to write, in any language; as the more advanced skill of manipulating the talents of reading and writing with sufficient proficiency to function normally within one's society (this is usually called functional literacy); or as a living relationship between the skills of reading and writing and the best thought of a particular culture. Each of these definitions has an inherent bias that may distort the results of the studies in which it is used. Both the simple and the functional definition of literacy tacitly assume that there exists a mechanical relation between the skills of reading and writing and social development. This underlying assumption gives birth in underdeveloped nations to literacy campaigns and education drives. There is no prima facie reason to make this assumption, however, and in fact a new generation of social historians is now busily engaged in proving that no such relation exists. Their labors, unfortunately, are like their predecessors' in being fixated on the single issue of whether literacy contributes to the growth of civilization. Only their answer differs.

Those who define literacy as a meeting of mechanical skill and cultivated thought invariably speak in defense of a particular class or ideology. Their definitions assume that cultivated thought is thought such as they think. Aristocrats and professors are especially given to this sort of definition, although in fairness we should note that each of the three definitions contains an ideological bias. Each assumes to varying degrees that those who cannot meet a standard of literacy are ignorant and unwashed, and, conversely, that the ignorant and unwashed are illiterate by the given standard. This hidden tautology is clearly demonstrable in tests of functional literacy, in which the victim is asked questions about his ability to fill out unemployment forms, make use of food stamps, and understand his legal rights if arrested. Not surprisingly, tests of this sort discover that the so-called functionally illiterate are unemployed, on welfare, and criminally inclined. These tests foreshadow their answers in their questions. It happens that many professors who applied for unemployment after the recent closing of a small college were rejected for failure to complete their forms properly.

And even Supreme Court justices disagree about the meaning of an accused man's rights. A little more caution is necessary before consigning large segments of the population to the prepacked category of functional illiteracy. In their haste, many students of literacy have simply assumed the conclusion demanded by their *idée fixe:* that lack of reading and writing skills is correlated to poor social development.

Once the researcher has arrived at a definition of literacy, he will then seek evidence to establish how many people in a given time and place possess it. This, at least, ought to be the practice. In fact, many social historians simply reverse this procedure and define literacy to suit the data available to them. The clearest instance of this habit is among students of reading and writing skills in England before the modern era. Since a number of court papers and political petitions survive from the seventeenth and eighteenth centuries, some social historians define literacy as the ability to sign one's name to these documents. From these researches telling conclusions about the origins of the industrial age and the rise of literacy are sometimes drawn—unwisely.

Those who have an interest in reading and writing skills in periods from which few or no signatures survive are compelled to rely on whatever snippets of information they can find—such as Thomas More's or the bishop of Winchester's comments—on figures about the number of schools and students in them, and on anecdotal material from literature and tradition. Wills, if they survive, often provide information about the presence of books in various types of household, but, for the most part, before the nineteenth century, we are safer to speak of literacy in generalizations rather than in figures. The figures as well as the definitions must always be suspect.

The point of assembling figures about the technologies of literacy is sometimes purely informational, as in a census count, but more often to assert a causal relation between them and some element of social or individual development. The notion that there is some connection between development and literacy is by now a commonplace. This notion is perfectly valid if literacy is properly defined but dangerously misleading where it is not. Problems arise chiefly where literacy is defined simply as the possession of mechanical skills in reading and writing.

We should note first that the simple diffusion of reading and writing skills does not dictate any particular political, economic, or social forms. In the first Christian century Rome had a population well-versed in reading and writing. It was a military autocracy with little trace of our modern industrial economy. Iceland in the eighteenth century achieved near total diffusion of reading and writing skills among its population (it can still claim the highest ratio of bookstores to citizens in the world). It is a pacific democracy whose economy depends on fishing and agriculture, not heavy industry as in the developed nations of Europe. In Bangladesh or Haiti, it is true, the absence of reading or writing skills in the population correlates nicely with terrifically low figures of per capita income and economic development; however, in 1978 at least six out of every ten Saudi Arabians probably could not read or write while the gross national product of Saudi Arabia, if distributed per capita, was $8,040 (by comparison, the same figure in Britain for that year was $5,030). Obviously, reading and writing skills alone do not determine the course of a nation's development, nor does their absence prevent an economy from prospering where natural resources are intelligently exploited. Reading and writing are neither necessary nor sufficient causes of economic prosperity.

Reading and writing may, however, be necessary factors in certain types of economic development, especially in those economies that cannot rely on easily exportable minerals but must instead depend on technology and industrialization in order to extract value from their natural situations. This premise has become an axiom upon which much modern developmental and educational strategy, both in third-world countries and in economically advanced nations, is based. Unfortunately, however, much current thinking regards literacy solely as the mechanical adoption of reading and writing skills, and asserts that, once acquired, these skills will produce similar economic and spiritual benefits throughout the world. This view, it seems clear, is too simple.

Two studies, one done in Bombay for UNESCO, the other conducted in what was then East Pakistan by a team of American researchers, typify the thinking surrounding the axiom that reading and writing are necessary to industrial or technological development. The Bombay study compared a group of factory workers who could read and write with a similar group that could not. On average, the readers and writers earned more money, and when both groups were evaluated by their supervisors, the readers and writers were without exception rated better at handling complex machinery or skilled jobs. The supervisors lopsidedly favored the readers and writers in every category of performance. They were better at maintaining equipment, reporting damage, and learning new skills. They had fewer accidents than the non-readers, came to work more promptly, and wasted less time talking at work. Unquestionably, the man who can read and write is a better worker than the one who cannot.

But is he a better worker because he has learned to read and write or has he learned to read and write because he is a better worker? In an economy where the supervisors have an unmistakable prejudice in favor of readers as employees, the wise man learns how to read. His wisdom precedes his acquisition of this skill, and it is his wisdom, not his reading, that finally gets him the job. The canny man who has divined the bias of his employer is naturally a better worker than the dolt who has not. This objection is at least possible and may be applied against most claims that reading and writing are necessary talents for development. In the Bombay study, the important but unasked question is whether the supervisors' prejudice in favor of readers and writers is well founded in the abstract. In India, where the English economy has been the model for development, it is not surprising to find a prejudice in favor of the same skills possessed by most English workers in the nineteenth and early twentieth centuries, when England was the most industrialized nation in the world. The question, then, is: Does the English model of literacy skills and development apply universally?

Before attempting to answer this question, let us ask another that arises from the study done in East Pakistan. There, reading and writing skills were found to be positively correlated with a broadening of political and intellectual horizons. While the non-reader typically identified himself as a member of a family or village, the reader more often thought of himself as a citizen of a nation or other large group. Other studies have likewise claimed that readers and writers are more adept at abstract thinking.

Once again, these studies do not tell us whether men have broader horizons because they learn to read or if they learn to read because they have broader horizons. They leave the impression that a knowledge of reading and writing is magical in its effects, transforming primitive villagers into global citizens. These studies also fail to ask: Where did these men learn the mechanics of literacy? and How much influence has the process of learning, as opposed to the skill itself, had on their thinking?

THE IRANIAN EXAMPLE

A partial response to both questions can be found in the example of Iran, a country that holds a special place in the history of literacy. At the beginning of this century, Iran had a typically low level of reading and writing skills among the general population. As in medieval Europe, most instruction in these arts was conducted by and in the service of the controlling religious interests—in the Iranian case, Koranic schools educated some small fraction of the population. With the accession of the Palevi family, however, Iran embarked upon an aggressive educational campaign designed to foster the broadest dissemination of reading and writing skills, especially among city dwellers. This campaign was so well supported and so conscientiously waged by the state that in the era of the United Nations and under the leadership of the late Shah Mohammed Palevi, Iran became a center for world literacy programs. UNESCO held a series of conferences on literacy in Teheran, where a permanent literacy group was established. The Shah himself was unstinting in his commitment to local and global attempts to spread the talents of reading and writing: "The increasing use of machinery and technology demands a rising level of intelligence. The better our instruments become, the more skilled technicians we need to operate them, engineers to build them, inventors to perfect them. Against such a background it hardly needs recalling that illiteracy involves an inadmissible wasting of intellectual energy for the whole of mankind." So said the Shah to a conference of educators in 1965. His sentiments express the widely held opinion that reading and writing skills are mechanical and endow their possessors with the basic talents with which to meet the challenges of Western technology.

But Iran itself is eloquent witness that this mechanical approach to reading and writing will not do. By 1975 Iran had achieved a so-called literacy rate of about 70 percent of the population, an extraordinarily high level of skill in the Middle East. By 1978 the Shah was deposed by a puritanical Islamic reaction. The Shah and his father had hoped, as most purveyors of reading and writing skills do, that training in the arts possessed by men in the developed areas of the world—specifically reading and writing—would perforce lead to Western habits of thought and patterns of productivity. They were wrong.

The mechanical skills of reading and writing always react with the prevailing attitude toward language of the culture into which they are introduced, with results specific to that culture. In Iran the prevailing attitude toward language is inextricably bound up with the religion of the people. The Persian believes that ultimate truth and the deployment of language are intimately related, in ways which, while they might have been intelligible to Europeans of Plato's or Milton's time, are now alien to the thought of Westerners. Bruce Laingen, the American chargé d'affaires in Iran before and during the hostage crisis, wrote to Washington in 1979 to explain the peculiar psychology of the Iranians. "The Persian proclivity for assuming that to say something is to do it further complicates matters," he said. His report, which seems to have been ignored by the State Department, testifies to the existence of a native literacy in Iran that fundamentally separates Iran from the Western countries it had tried to emulate under the Shah.

In Iran, attempts to modernize the orthography and grammar of Parsi in order to create a simple and efficient vehicle of communication naturally encountered stiff opposition from scholars and clerics. The prophet himself was reputed to have said that the ink of the scholar was more esteemed than the blood of the martyr. Where the population at large believes such an adage, it will be impossible to convince them even in generations that reading and writing ought to be regarded primarily as tools of economic advantage. Reading and writing will either be confined to the care of a learned elite or else they will be endowed with a sanctity and purpose unknown in the West. Illustrative of the first case are the northern Iranian peasants who agreed to learn reading and writing only on condition that they be paid for their efforts. Among them these skills had been practiced only by a special class of educated men, whose monopoly they saw no reason to break except for payment. The second situation is illustrated by the late premier, now martyred, of Khomeni's revolutionary Iran, Ali Rajai, who rose to power from the position of provincial schoolteacher. In such a culture, the village schoolteacher is no mere purveyor of functional skills or information. He is a man entrusted with a sacred mystery.

Small wonder that the Iranian revolutionaries and the American diplomats had such difficulty in speaking to one another. Both parties undoubtedly possessed the mechanical skills of reading and writing. In most instances, they even had English in common. Americans, however, regard language as a functional device for conveying information and asserting practical obligations, while the Iranians considered the spokesmen for the Great Satan to be crass liars oblivious to the import of language. Two such groups may speak the same language and use it with the same mechanical skills, but they can hardly be said to be literate in the same way.

In the study conducted in East Pakistan, workers who could read and write identified with larger units than those who could not. The villager who reads also sees himself as a citizen of a nation and a member of the world community, and the implication of the study is that he is therefore a more civilized individual. This conclusion has little support in reality. Of course the man who has learned to read has contact with information that comes from beyond the horizons of his village or tribe, and he might naturally feel himself to be a participant in a larger nexus of events than those to which he had formally been accustomed. But the expansion of horizons does nothing to increase tolerance or wisdom. Reading may stimulate the Asian or African to contemplate events beyond his immediate neighborhood, but he is likely to approach these events just as he does those within his more limited native community. If the Shah taught the Iranians to read and write, he failed nonetheless to overcome their parochial and traditional religious and political sentiments. Reading itself, taught without any further training of the mind, is merely a skill that increases the amount of information available to the student, which permits him to project his existing cultural attitudes onto national or global events. This phenomenon is as likely to lead to violence and misunderstanding as to universal harmony and understanding, for new readers will judge the complex machinations of modern civilization by the same standards that they apply in their traditional communities. The mobs of Teheran or the guerrilla bands of the PLO contain large numbers of readers and writers, if we can trust the statistics for these populations. Their mechanical skills have not served to temper their cultural predispositions.

Earlier, the Bombay study provoked the question, does the English model of reading and writing apply universally? The answer is clearly that it does not. Any relation between reading and writing skills and economic development along Western lines is highly doubtful. What is certain is that each culture will produce its own brand of literacy. The mechanical habits of reading and writing may play a part in the literacy of any culture, but the existing attitude toward language will determine that part.

Attitudes toward language are not the only variable that will affect campaigns to spread the skills of reading and writing. The way these skills are taught and their intended employment obviously have their impact as well. In the sixteenth and seventeenth centuries in Britain and its American colonies, many learned to read so that they might have access to the Scriptures. Their literacy was therefore intimately connected with a critical and interpretative function, and, not surprisingly, these readers and writers formed an articulate backbone to dissenting and revolutionary movements. But their literacy is a very different phenomenon from the kind of literacy examined in the Bombay study I have mentioned. There, supervisors praised literate workmen for reasons such as "avoiding discussions while at work and avoiding waste of time by proper planning" and having "good relations with supervisors, co-workers, and cooperative behavior." Seventeenth-century Anglo-Saxon literacy at least had the potential of making a man dangerous by his new powers of critical application. Twentieth-century developmental literacy is usually intended to make men harmless, obedient, and productive. Once again, the skills of reading and writing have very little inherent influence. Their effects largely depend on the ideological context in which they are acquired.

THE PSYCHOLOGICAL BURDEN OF ILLITERACY

Increased social efficiency and obedience, largely benefiting the established order, are among both the chief causes and the chief effects of the general spread of reading and writing skills in modern developed or developing economies. Equally important but less easy to grasp is the psychological pressure that stimulates the universal diffusion of reading and writing. Perhaps this phenomenon is best understood through a letter taken from the mighty social mirror of Ann Landers's column.

Dear Ann:
   I have been reading you since I was in junior high. It seems I've grown up with Ann Landers. I remember a column a long time ago about a woman who discovered she had married a man who couldn't read even though he graduated from high school.
   At the time I thought it was funny. I also wondered how such a thing could happen. Well, now I know, because it has happened to me.
   I went with this man (I'll call him John) for six months. He grew up on a farm in Vermont, loves nature

and animals—as I do—and is very kind. We have a good marriage.

John does construction work, and I am a secretary-bookkeeper. To make a long story short, I began to notice he never read a newspaper, magazine, or book and had trouble with signs, directions and even labels. His excuse was he couldn't see the small print.

Yesterday John admitted the truth. He can't read. He was so ashamed he cried. How can I help him, Ann? Now that I know, I feel it is *our* problem.

One of Your Flock

John certainly has a handicap in his inability to read. He cannot understand labels, signs, or newspapers. Yet as the letter demonstrates, his handicap is hardly catastrophic. He is a fine husband with a good job who has managed to reach a productive stage of adulthood without apparently suffering any more than minimal inconvenience from his incapacity. He had been married some time before even his wife noticed that he had a problem. There is every indication that John is a decent, law-abiding citizen, even though he can't read the laws he abides by. In the course of modern society, John's life would have been different in many more of its details had he been unable to drive or operate machinery, skills which one assumes that he does have as a farmboy and construction worker.

John's or his wife's reaction to his handicap, however, is by no means as balanced and understanding as ours may be as casual observers. John has guarded his guilty secret for years, and when the domestic revelation finally comes, he weeps. His wife is so confused and upset that she turns to Ann Landers to save them. Ann's typically sensible answer suggested that for people like John, "someone who cares will do them the biggest favor of their lives and let them know there are free services throughout the country for teaching adult non-readers." Practical, yes, but even Ann sees non-readers in a highly dramatic light. "The biggest favor of their lives"?

The shame that John and his wife endure reveals the high emotional value that possession of reading and writing skills has come to have in developed and now in developing societies. The man who cannot read or write is today in the West considered unfinished, uncivilized, perhaps even inhuman, a social judgment that may be, as in John's case, widely disproportionate to the loss he suffers through his inability. But in assigning such psychological importance to the arts of reading and writing, society does not consult only its reason. The non-reader commits the same kind of offense against the social order as the man who eats his peas with a knife or picks his nose in public places. He breaks one of the filaments of collective behavior. The man who eats peas with a knife demonstrates his ignorance of or indifference to the habits of his neighbors and can expect to be ostracized from the main stream of social life; he is called uncouth. The man who cannot read or write similarly lacks one of the habits equated, rightly or wrongly, with acceptable social behavior; he is called stupid. He too can expect ostracism. A recent study goes so far as to suggest that some young blacks fail to learn reading and writing as a studied attack upon the society that demands these skills of them as part of its definition of minimal human behavior. This suggestion illuminates the tremendous importance of the psychology of literacy, and is almost certainly correct.

The psychological importance of literacy goes a long way toward explaining the swift expansion of reading and writing skills in the general population of the West. The best evidence indicates that Shakespeare's father could not write. He became a magistrate in Stratford nonetheless and witnessed official documents with a cross or a mark signifying a pair of compasses. At some time between Shakespeare's day and our own, however, society has come to demand reading and writing as minimal educational skills in its citizens, and a magistrate today who could not sign his name would be a scandal. In England this psychological pressure began to have a telling effect in the nineteenth century, when we find workers whose livelihoods do not depend on them nevertheless expending precious time and money to acquire mechanical habits of literacy. Their ambition can hardly have been to rise to high office or great wealth. They wanted the psychological satisfaction of participating in the social activities then considered essential within their society's definition of ordinary human accomplishments. Even before compulsory education, over 60 percent of Englishmen knew how to read and write. By the time of the Great War, failure to have these talents would have set a man apart as a social cripple.

The psychological importance attached to the mechanical skills of literacy in the West is connected with their ability to promote social obedience and efficiency. The man who can neither read nor write is a weak link in the information chain that unites society by a constant flow of announcements and directives. Such men are dangerous. Conformity is essential to modern, developed societies. Without it industrial economies could not provide us with the material blessings of scientific knowledge. A widely diffused knowledge of reading and writing is necessary for the maintenance of order and is therefore one of the foundations on which our prosperity rests. But the psychological pressure to acquire these skills is maintained by the ideology that tells us mechanical language skills and rational participation in the affairs of our culture go hand in hand. Our society makes someone like John feel deficient as a thinking human being because he cannot read or write when in fact it wants him to possess these skills the better to integrate him into a vast nexus of impersonal economic forces over which he will have no rational control and about which he will be discouraged from thinking critically.

I have stressed the aspects of mechanical literacy that foster social obedience and depend for their wide dispersal on a strong psychological fixation upon their attainment as necessary ingredients of civilized life. These aspects of literacy are not particularly uplifting, but they are important to keep in mind as we contemplate development in the emerging economies of Asia, Africa, and South America. By insisting upon the spread of reading and writing skills in these economies as a precondition for successful development, we in the already developed West impose our own particular experience of literacy upon the world as a rigid rule of historical growth. Out of our own deeply felt psychological need for the mechanics of literacy, we preach the dissemination of reading and writing with missionary zeal, while we are often oblivious to those dimensions of literacy that, far from encouraging the spread of freedom and knowledge, merely support the grinding obedience and efficiency demanded by totalitarian regimes everywhere.

The statistics supporting the conclusion that universal mechanical literacy is necessary for economic development are everywhere flawed by the Western prejudice of the observers who prepare them, and they are open to numerous conflicting interpretations. Statistics of this sort must always be subject to the most careful and skeptical scrutiny. Several social historians have even cast a gloomy eye over the English experience of mass literacy and concluded that the spread of basic mechanical skills coincided with a decline in social mobility and a growing incidence of a sense of alienation among the working classes. The highest rates of alcoholism and suicide are to be found not in the developing nations but in the developed economies where reading and writing skills are nearly universal.

Even if it is true that the traditional view of reading and writing as the foundation of liberty and progress is seriously flawed, I think it is also true that there is nothing about these talents in themselves that leads directly to self-destructive despair. The peasant who learns to read does not instantly become either a factory worker or an alcoholic. Instead he gains a skill that makes all the woes of modern life readily accessible to him along with all its advantages. By having this skill he is more easily integrated into the routines of a modern economy—a burden that may be all the harder for him to bear if he has been taught reading or writing without any collateral training in the intricacies of language, for he will find himself capable of new obedience and efficiency but impotent to deal with the strange emotions evoked by the modern condition.

THE PRISONER PHENOMENON

Literacy, however, is generally credited with developing more than our economic potential. It is supposed to be a means of mental development as well. Let us call the supposed process by which literacy enlightens the individual mind and advances culture the "prisoner phenomenon." The most eloquent testimonials to the power of literacy are found in the memoirs of inmates: "I have often reflected upon the new vistas that reading opened to me. I knew right there in prison that reading had changed forever the course of my life. As I see it today, the ability to read awoke inside me some long dormant craving to be mentally alive." So Malcolm X explains his intellectual awakening while serving a sentence for robbery in the Norfolk Prison Colony in Massachusetts.

Malcolm X had no more than an eighth-grade education when he went to jail. He had nearly forgotten how to read and write. When Malcolm, in prison, first heard about the teaching of Elijah Muhammad, he could not because of his poor education correspond intelligently with the man he came to believe was a prophet. In frustration, Malcolm studied the dictionary, writing out each entry from A to Z in longhand. He soon graduated to reading American history and then philosophy—Socrates, Schopenhauer, Kant, Nietzsche. "Months passed without my even thinking about being imprisoned. In fact, up to then, I had never been so truly free in my life." The story of Malcolm X is an archetypal example of the way in which literacy redeems what is most vital in us from the chaos of ignorance. One of the most striking figures of American history was born out of this awakening in the Norfolk Prison Colony.

We are all prisoners of our ignorance. By opening new worlds of information and ideas for us, literacy is one of the chief means of human liberation. John Bunyan, Malcolm X, and centuries of prisoners whose minds have come alive from the touch of literacy bear witness to the almost mystical power of the Word to transform our lives. In this book, I have taken a skeptical line about the various powers usually ascribed to literacy, but I see no way out of the obvious lesson of the prisoner phenomenon: literacy can transform the mind and the life of man.

Since the prisoner phenomenon is a well-attested means of awakening the best in the human spirit, we may rightly ask how it comes about. Incarceration itself, it seems, is not sufficient to provoke it. Most prisoners in Attica or Leavenworth do not undergo the mental revolution Malcolm X describes. For the most part, those who do develop an interest in reading and writing use these improved talents not for the study of philosophy but for the manufacture of writs designed to shorten their terms of confinement. Our earlier observation that literacy is primarily a tool of practical advantage holds in prison as well as in society at large.

American high schools have tried for decades to reproduce the prisoner phenomenon in the classroom by making the educational experience resemble penal servitude as nearly as possible. Not only does the monotonous curriculum of high school mimic the routine of the jailhouse; high schools are also designed to look as if they were prisons, complete with fences, bars, bells, and wardens. In high school, too, the failure of incarceration alone to produce the prisoner phenomenon has been conspicuous. The percentage of high-school graduates who embrace literacy with the enthusiasm recorded by Malcolm X is probably (we lack statistics) no greater and may be less than the percentage of prisoners who do. The loss of freedom and dignity does not automatically compel a man to seek the liberating solace of the Word.

Neither did Malcolm become a passionate intellect because he could read Socrates. He read Socrates because he had a passionate intellect. First Malcolm heard his relatives speak of Elijah Muhammed. The curiosity engendered by this oral contact led Malcolm to undertake the arduous road to literacy and finally to the creation of his own movement. Once his passion had been aroused, literacy provided the means of developing and organizing it, but literacy did not—does not ever by itself—awaken the passion of the mind. In the fourth century Augustine changed the course of his life and thus of Western history when he took up a Bible in his mother's garden and discovered Christ. What led to this momentous confrontation with the Christian text was not literacy, but the voice of a child Augustine heard that urged him to "take up the book and read." Literacy can only alter our lives where some still small voice urges us on to seek change. This maxim helps explain why high-school graduates are often dull-witted even though they can read and write. No voice invites them to take up the book.

I wish I could explain why the desire for wisdom moves one man and not another—why one prisoner becomes Malcolm X while another remains a common felon. Literacy does not precede but follows some more fundamental movement of the will toward knowledge. In the first chapter of this book, I suggested that literacy is always a combination of consciousness about language and technical skill in the manipulation of the technologies of language. The prisoner phenomenon further elucidates this definition. Does the mind become more aware because it becomes literate or literate because it becomes more aware? In civilizations like our own, reading and writing—the technologies of literacy—are so closely tied to consciousness of language that this question is usually answered with the reassuring reply that reading and writing make better minds. I reject this reply on the basis of the prisoner phenomenon. Once awakened, consciousness may turn to literacy for fulfillment, but the awakening itself occurs beyond literacy. Here the study of literacy reaches one of its natural boundaries, beyond which lie the realms of metaphysics and psychology. The act that begins to lead us out of the prison of our ignorance is not reading or writing or any other technology of language, but some more primitive initiative toward consciousness. This act may not even be verbal, though words are finally its manifestation. The impulse toward consciousness underlies all literacy but is not itself literacy. It is the mysterious act of the mind in discovering itself.

CHAPTER SIX

Hopefully into the Future:
John Locke and Correct Usage

The spread of the mechanical skills of literacy is everywhere connected with the prevailing uses and ideas of language in the surrounding culture. Huge expenditure on Western training in basic skills will not convert a developing nation into a productive industrial economy where the native sense of the language defies technological applications. Successful development requires a widely held, pragmatic view of language, such as the English adopted at the dawn of the modern era. From the seventeenth century, England was specially favored for the growth of a modern economy by a shared sense that language is a medium of something called truth. Opinion might vary as to what truth is, but from Locke, to Dr. Johnson, to Mill and later in Browning and Tennyson—throughout the range of philosophy, social theory, and letters—language was for the Englishman endowed with purpose, practical or divine, but purpose with pragmatic and scientific validity in the daily affairs of life.

The common perspective of language as a medium of truth gave to developing England a solid and practicable literacy fit to go forth into the world and prosper. This literacy created a standard of correct English that facilitated the rise of our capitalist economy. The present chapter will look at Locke's brand of literacy and some of its modern mutations.

STANDARD USAGE AND THE
RISE OF CAPITALISM

British and American cultures have produced their own peculiar forms of literacy, which are sometimes regarded as the inevitable forms that literacy must take in societies where reading and writing are developed. This is not the case. Every instance of literacy should be treated individually.

The best evidence, based on the ability to sign documents, suggests that in seventeenth-century England the number of male readers and writers fluctuated between 25 and 40 percent of the population. Those raised during the disruptions of the revolution were more likely not to have learned reading and writing, while more stable conditions at the start of the century seem to have favored a somewhat higher rate. Of course, the 25 to 40 percent figure is deceptive because it covers men of all classes. David Cressy, the indefatigable historian of seventeenth-century English literacy, assures us that almost all members of the gentry and of the professional classes could read and write, while very few laborers could do so. Tradesmen usually could write—their business demanded paperwork and communication between towns—while agricultural workers usually could not.

Since historians commonly locate the origins of the English industrial revolution in the seventeenth century, figures like these are often brought forward to draw a connection between development and literacy. An often-quoted estimate has it that a literacy rate of approximately 40 percent in the population is a necessary condition for modern economic development. But this view is too simple, as the English example will show.

English literacy—or any other—cannot be understood simply as a matter of readers and writers. The quality of the literacy is far more important than mere numbers. Throughout English history a zeal for language is apparent, and this zeal must be reckoned into any account of English literacy. At the end of the seventeenth century, a London bookseller collected 23,000 books and pamphlets published between 1641 and 1662, the period of the revolution. If the population of England at this time was around five and a half million, and if the rate of readers and writers was about 35 percent of the male population, then at least for these twenty years one book was published for every forty-two readers. This high ratio of publication to audience reveals a population not only reading and writing, in the functional way the populations of modern developing nations learn to do, but reading and writing with enthusiasm in an atmosphere of ideas and debate. Many learned to read solely so they could have a firsthand experience of holy writ while others learned in order to further their economic ambitions. This was a society in which literacy was connected with the most stimulating agents of human development—religion and gain. The importance of religion and economics for English development has long been a subject of study, and here it is only important to note that literacy is not so much a cause of development as part of the familiar historical picture.

What is less familiar is the linkage of attitudes toward language, literacy, and development. A view of the uses of language emerged from the English seventeenth century that helped to determine the success of the industrial revolution and establish England for a time as the world's leading power. This view was a practical compromise between the attitudes of Donne and his party and of Bunyan and his. It takes its essential form in the philosophy of John Locke, who ought to be called the father of modern Anglo-American literacy. In Locke the opposed views of the schools I have represented by Donne and Bunyan were reconciled in a single type of literacy fitted for business, empire, and science.

For Locke as for Donne and the schoolmen before him, language was a complex vehicle of truth, "the great bond that holds society together, and the common conduit, whereby the improvements of knowledge are conveyed from one man and one generation to another." Because of its complex and ambiguous nature, language demands acute and constant application of human intelligence in its use. "Those who pretend seriously to search after or maintain truth, should think themselves obliged to study how they might deliver themselves without obscurity, doubtfulness, or equivocation." Locke agreed with the school of Donne that the truths of language only yield themselves to the fullest and most informed application of the human spirit. He only differed with them on what a full and informed undertaking might be. For the school of Donne, it had been a celebration and an imitation of the paradoxes of man's life and his relation to the divine. But for Locke, the truth that language contains is not divine but mundane, orderly, and practical. He is in the spirit of Donne by his demand that language be placed under the control of critical authority, but he is a modern in the spirit of Descartes in so far as he insists this authority must be rational—and initially devoid of any reference to God or tradition. When a man uses words, "their signification, in his use of them, is limited to his ideas, and they can be signs of nothing else."

Locke's dictum that the authority set over the interpretation of language must be rational also gives him common ground with Bunyan and the believers in the primacy of the Word. For Locke language is an intensely personal experience. Its final validity rests on nothing but the mind of the user. Of course, Locke does not accept the other premise of Bunyan's school, that God informs the Word in both its propagation and its comprehension. This is always the first premise of the man who preaches the holy and democratic power of the Word, and Locke rejects it. Yet his philosophy still insists on the notion that language is primarily a personal revelation. Thus Locke combines two broad and different ideas of language in his system, altering both by depriving them of any reference beyond mind itself.

Locke is one of that handful of philosophers whose influence on culture has been obvious and palpable. His great work, the *Essay Concerning Human Understanding*, was a huge success in his lifetime. For a hundred years after his death his thought was the point of departure for other philosophers, not only in England but on the continent as well. His success should be attributed not so much to his introduction of a new idea, but to his synthesis of apparently contradictory views. This synthesis immediately and spontaneously recommended itself to the spirit of the people and the age.

Certainly the philosophy of Locke goes a long way toward helping us understand the literacy of England in the age of development, but it is one of the curiosities of social history that during the eighteenth century, as England continued to develop into the world's first industrial power, the percentage of readers and writers in the population actually seems to have fallen, and the number of books published also declined from the rate established in the turbulent seventeenth century. This apparent decline in literacy continued into the early years of the nineteenth century, when a dramatic increase in both the number of readers and texts took place, culminating in our modern industrial civilization with its universal diffusion of reading and writing skills and its heaps of printed materials. There are many excellent reasons for the decline of reading skills and printing in the period immediately after Locke. For instance, economic factors forced the price of books up. Class lines were more strictly observed; the role of reading as a vehicle of social mobility was reduced. The explanations, however, do not tell us how it was possible to lay the foundations of the modern developed state in the face of these declines, especially when the common wisdom maintains that literacy skills and development proceed together. The problem is all the more vexing when we consider that in our imagination, at any rate, the English eighteenth century produced a model "literate" culture. This, after all, was the age of Pope and Swift, Gibbon and Butler, Fielding and Dr. Johnson.

The English eighteenth century is remarkable not for the quantity of its literacy, but for its quality. The philosophy of Locke embodies an attitude toward language that is fitted for worldly success. Its emphasis on the highly personal nature of language grows out of and reinforces a society that stresses individual initiative, and its demand for clarity and precision of thought facilitates practical communication of all kinds, whether scientific or commercial. Of course, Locke's notions were as much the product as they were the cause of these cultural forces. The rise of scientific thought made Locke's views possible, and to some extent the advent of printing was the vehicle for the rise of scientific thought, as Elizabeth Eisenstein has shown in her history of print. Still, Locke is cause as well as effect. He freed language by severing its connections with theology. He demanded that standards of precision and clarity be universally applied to all language, and he himself wrote in English, not in the scientific Latin of Newton's *Principia*. It may be true that the spread of reading and writing skills halted or even receded in the eighteenth century, but the substantial minority that could read and write did so with an amazingly uniform and purposeful sense of the practical advantages of language.

This is the era of the debate over the creation of an English Academy to protect good usage of the mother tongue and the period of the first great English dictionary. "It is not enough," Locke had said, "that men have ideas, determined ideas, for which they make signs stand; but they must also take care to apply their words as near as may be to such ideas as common use has annexed to them." More important to English development than sheer numbers of readers and writers was the shared notion among those who could read and write that the language was a commonly held medium for the exchange of ideas and information that had ultimate value for the practical improvement of life.

A related development of this shared appreciation of the uses of language was the rise of the doctrine of correct usage. Queen Anne scolded one of her diplomats for atrocious spelling, just as Augustus had cashiered one of his administrators for his solecisms. The Renaissance had allowed a wonderful freedom in spelling and grammar, but the eighteenth century, convinced that the advantages possible by the use of language could only be obtained by the most perfect clarity, insisted upon commonly sanctioned forms of language in order to promote utility. The rules of English grammar and spelling that are routinely taught in modern schoolrooms were largely codified in this period. What is more, they were insisted upon as essential accomplishments for any educated person. In his dictionary, Dr. Johnson defined grammar as the "science of speaking correctly," and he cites Locke to sustain his definition. At the heart of Johnson's great lexicographic effort was a desire to fulfill the need diagnosed by the author of the *Essay Concerning Human Understanding:* to provide one correct form for English as proof against "the corruptions of ignorance and the caprices of innovation," as Johnson says in his preface to the Dictionary. Language conceived in this way is both the symptom of and the vehicle for a culture embarked on a scientific view of the world. Dr. Johnson, who has the reputation of a literary curmudgeon, was wholly conscious of the scientific import of his work: "but I shall not think my employment useless or ignoble, if by my assistance foreign nations, and distant ages, gain access to the propagators of knowledge, and understand the teachers of truth; if my labours afford light to the repositories of science, and add celebrity to Bacon, to Hooker, to Milton, and to Boyle." In the Doctor's list, science stands shoulder to shoulder with epic verse. Speaking of the uses of language in the age of Johnson, the contemporary French philosopher Foucault points out that the function of what he calls "classical discourse" was *to ascribe a name to things, and in that name to name their being.*" A correct and authoritative language was essential for this endeavor, in order that the universe could be reduced to manageable and manipulable proportions within the framework of words.

The danger of any doctrine of correct usage is that it will arrest the course of the language upon which it is imposed and create an artificial language of power divorced from the thought of the people, as had happened in the Roman empire and in the medieval Church. That there is a danger is only now being realized in the Anglo-American community, but the eighteenth century did not shrink from the creation of correct and artificial forms. In fact, the thinkers of the period, following Locke, regarded it as an obligation to establish mutual intelligibility by erecting common linguistic formulas, and it is not too farfetched to say that the industrial prosperity of England relied in some measure on their sense of correct usage. The eighteenth century fitted out the language for precision in the transmittal of information and clarity in the propagation of individual desires—two necessary ingredients for the language that would become the mother tongue of the industrial revolution and the British empire.

What the English experience of literacy in the eighteenth century tells us about twentieth-century literacy for developing nations is not that the masses must all learn to read and write, but that the powerful minorities of a nation that do possess the mechanical skills of literacy should also share a practical sense of the application of language. They need not be dedicated to the philosophy of Locke, but need only have a common understanding about language that admits of practical application. Iranian development has in part been thwarted by the absence of this shared pragmatic sense among the educated minority, and development in modern China faces a similar difficulty. Mass diffusion of reading and writing skills may follow from this initial ideological pragmatism, but mass diffusion in itself seems inessential to successful development, even though the universal dissemination of these talents might provide numerous emotional and economic benefits to their individual possessors, a premise we will soon have to examine.

Locke's philosophy in the period of empire and development fostered a scientific, capitalistic use of language, but also supported a highly individualistic, moral notion that was closely connected with Bunyan's literacy. For Locke, language is before anything else the means by which the mind makes ideas known to itself. "Words," he says, "in their primary or immediate signification, stand for nothing but the *ideas in the mind of him that uses them.*" Language is the means of self-realization, and only later, when the private forms of language are correlated with those used by other men, is it a vehicle of social knowledge and action. Like Bunyan, Locke has a sense of language as intimate and immediate, except that he does not see the deity brooding over its immediacy. Nonetheless, there remains in Locke and in Dr. Johnson after him a sense in which language is more than an arbitrary series of personal or social conventions. If it is not connected with God, it is still the essential tool for the discovery of truth. For Locke, "those who pretend seriously to search after or maintain truth" must practice their use of language. For Johnson, the dictionary was a key to "the teachers of truth." The better a man knows the habits and skills of language in this view, the closer he is to a personal knowledge of the truths of the universe.

THE LIBERAL FALLACY:
TRUTH, PROGRESS, AND LITERACY

This doctrine of language, derived in part from the ancient celebration of it as a manifestation of the Word, has helped over the last 200 years to stimulate an intense desire in the West to master the skills of language. We think thereby to make ourselves masters of truth. Locke's theory of language connects skill in the manipulation of language with rational knowledge of the truths of life. This equation has had immense importance in shaping the West's psychological and economic devotion to the cause of mass literacy.

In the last century, Robert Owen, the social visionary noted for his utopian industrial settlements, stated the principles behind the mass diffusion of reading and writing skills in his usual succinct fashion. Owen declared that in the ideal state all children will be educated, and thereby enabled to "know themselves, and what humanity is, through a knowledge of the unchanging laws of God. By children being enabled to ascertain this knowledge for themselves, *through an accurate investigation of the facts* on which the knowledge is based, their minds will be made rational, which no minds have ever yet been" (Owen's italics). In Owen the peculiar tradition of English literacy is apparent. He is as much a believer in inspiration and the Word as Bunyan. In his utopia, however, language does not fill men with the Holy Ghost, but with Locke's rationality. Only let each man have the tools of reading and writing by which to gain access to the facts, and they will become models of reason.

Owen made his visionary claim in 1849. By then the diffusion of the skills of literacy was well under way. After hovering around 30 percent throughout the eighteenth century, the number of readers and writers in the English population began to rise steeply after 1800 at the same time that the new industrial cities were building in the English Midlands. By the end of the nineteenth century Britain had committed itself to the universal male franchise and had instituted a system of universal education. By the time of the Great War over 90 percent of English men and women could read and write—or so the statistics say.

"Universal teaching must precede universal enfranchisement," John Stuart Mill wrote in 1861. His observation is based on the same logic that guided Owen in forming his utopian concept of universal education. Only an intelligent electorate can make intelligent decisions, and the way to make the electorate intelligent is to provide it with the tools by which men reason—primarily, reading and writing. "I regard it as wholly inadmissible that any person should participate in the suffrage without being able to read, write, and I will add, perform the common operations of arithmetic," Mill said. Here, in essence, is the theory that mastery of the three R's is the royal road to reasonable thought and, beyond that, to democratic liberty. Mill's essay *On Liberty* is built on the unstated premise that in a free society, where the flow of ideas is unchecked and the populace has access through reading and writing to these ideas, the truth will eventually triumph because in the end men will be reasonable about ideas once they have had the opportunity to scrutinize them. We might note that Mill, like Owen, is firmly in the tradition of the eighteenth century. His theory provides for the victory of truth over falsehood— a complex phenomenon for him, certainly, but nonetheless an obtainable reality, all the more safely gained by extending a mechanical knowledge of language skills broadly throughout the population.

Noble as this theory of liberty is, it must be rejected as unreliable. Nothing in experience indicates that possession of the mechanical skills of reading and writing automatically confers political wisdom, advances human rationality, or leads on to truth. As has often been pointed out, Nazi Germany was one of the most educationally advanced nations on earth, and the dissemination of reading and writing skills must have been nearly universal.

Similarly, the totalitarian regime that currently operates the Soviet Union takes immense pride in its efforts on behalf of literacy. According to Soviet figures 99.7 percent of their citizens are literate, that is, know how to read and write and have a number of years of elementary education. Observers outside of Russia are agreed that these figures are a fraud, but they are interesting nonetheless because they indicate that basic education and political oppression are not natural enemies. The Russians are eager to disseminate reading and writing skills and even more eager to have the world believe they have already succeeded. The distinguished social historian Lawrence Stone once wrote that "modernizing tyrannies, however terrible they may be in the short run, carry with them the seeds of their own destruction, because of their inescapable emphasis on mass education and rapid university expansion in order to achieve industrial and military power." This widely held view is not, I think, tenable. The masses of the Soviet Union have shown no inclination to rise up because of their education. Traditional religious and national ties may threaten the domestic unity of the Communist state, but there is little evidence that the masses, with their mechanical literacy skills, have analyzed the Marxist idea and found it wanting. Lenin himself acknowledged that "literacy alone is not enough; we need the culture which teaches how to fight red tape and bribery." The Soviet regime has been both careful and clever in denying this culture, which is the soul of genuine literacy.

Thus we obtain the following postulate: there is no guarantee that because people can read and write they can also think. The British commanders of the Great War seem to have concurred in this gloomy postulate. One writer maintains that, leading an army drawn from a male population among which basic educational skills were said to be universal, they hesitated to order any maneuver more complex than a deadly frontal assault from the trenches because they doubted the ability of the average soldier to comprehend or execute a more exacting operation.

But if Locke's and Mill's doctrine of a connection between mechanical language skills and rationality has failed in reality, it has nonetheless proven very durable both as a theory and as a psychologically appealing tenet of ideology. As a theory it has lent a patina of nobility to the methods by which reading and writing skills are exploited in the world's economies. As a tenet of ideology it has become an important psychological tool for disciplining the populations of developed and developing nations.

The sudden and finally universal diffusion of reading and writing skills in England began near the start of the nineteenth century. The process has been mirrored in the development of other Western industrial economies and today is under way in the developing third world. It has other causes besides the desire by these nations for a rational electorate. These causes may generally be understood under two headings: the social need for increased efficiency and obedience on the part of a newly industrialized nation, and the psychological need of the people themselves for the sense of belonging that reading and writing provide.

The chief social boon that mass education in the basic mechanics of literacy affords is the more rapid and efficient transfer of information. This function of literacy need have no relation to any humane or civilizing objective on the part of the culture affected. The factory owner who puts up the sign "If you don't come in Sunday don't come in Monday" obviously expects that his employees can read. At the same time, he hopes that their talent for reading will only inspire speedy conformation to his dictates, not dialogues on resistance.

I think the factory owner's hope is realistic. Higgins, one of the working-class characters in Elizabeth Gaskell's *North and South*, a novel written in 1855 that examines the industrialization of nineteenth-century England, says at one point in the story that a supervisor at his mill once tried to convince him of the folly of unions by giving him a book on economics. "Come, I'll see what these chaps has got to say, and try if it's them or me as is th' noodle," says Higgins, who with other millions of the English working class had recently learned to read: "So I took th' book and tugged at it; but, Lord bless yo', it went on about capital and labour, and labour and capital, till it fair sent me off to sleep. I ne'er could rightly fix i' my mind which was which; and it spoke on 'em as if they was vartues or vices; and what I wanted for to know were the rights o' men, whether they were rich or poor—so be they only were men."

Higgins's ability to read has given him neither the taste nor the talent to appreciate complex ideas. Instead he wants to know a universal fact: what his rights are. Mrs. Gaskell's portrait of working-class literacy is shrewd. Without collateral training of some sort in the evaluation of thought and the problems of language, the man who has learned to read and write is generally fitted only for the more speedy comprehension and use of information. The advantages to an economy of this sort of literacy are apparent. They go a long way toward explaining the rapid dissemination of reading and writing skills at the dawn of the great age of factories. Business and government have much to gain and little to lose from a working class trained to understand written instructions and published notices, and at the same time this skill recommends itself to workers themselves as an accomplishment necessary for economic survival. The apparent risk run by the establishment—that reading will not only improve efficiency but introduce workers to dissident thought and provide them a means of organization—is in fact negligible because reading or writing in itself is a neutral talent incapable of effectuating change without some further training. The powers-that-be can in fact increase efficiency and obedience simultaneously not by resisting popular education, but by controlling it to ensure that only the brand of literacy of which it approves is taught. Hence the enthusiasm demonstrated by totalitarian states for high reading rates and mass education. The literacy programs operating on the model of the pioneer Brazilian educator Paolo Freire are also guided by the principle of obedience. In these, the uneducated are trained to read and write within the context of a socialist dialogue. The teachers profess to be liberating the mind. We may be certain that they are in fact accustoming it to accept orders within a socialist framework.

There are, of course, men in all classes and times who will use the skills of reading and writing to challenge ideas and menace authority. But these skills in themselves are not sufficient to produce those results. If they were, then bureaucrats and professors would always be revolutionary classes, while we know they are usually stodgy reactionaries even in those social settings where they are clearly exploited. In English history, we must ask whether those nineteenth-century working-class heroes who thrived on the likes of Ruskin's *Unto This Last* were militantly intelligent because they read or whether they read because they were militantly intelligent. My guess is that even without the mechanics of literacy they would have found a leading place in the popular armies of Wat Tyler or Oliver Cromwell.

The great danger posed to a state by the universal spread of mechanical literacy is not that men will suddenly recognize exploitation—some men have always recognized it without reading or writing and most have ignored it in spite of

these talents—but that the same habits of obedience and efficiency that these basic skills inculcate in a population may be
used not to further but to attack the established order. The
factory owner who puts up that "Don't come in Monday"
sign has little cause to fear that his employees, because they
can read, are secretly perusing Marx, but he may be certain
that if they can read his sign, they can also read the one announcing a meeting to form a union. The rapid transmittal of
information can work two ways, as the modern state has been
quick to see. The British and American governments at the
moment make little or no attempt to regulate the flow of
ideas, because they can be sure that ideas will be read by
few and understood by fewer. But information is a different
story. All governments are wary of the unrestricted exchange
of data. The law that governs English publishing is the Official Secrets Act, whereby the government limits the flow of
facts. In America, recent first-amendment cases of note have
dealt with the publication not of radical ideas but of dangerous information prejudicial to faith in government or the
established order. The Pentagon papers and the how-to-
build-an-H-bomb cases are examples. The sensible government, faced with universal mechanical literacy, fears facts,
not thoughts. Its population, while insensible to ideas, will
have been trained to respond to data.

On the whole, however, the benefits of social order and
efficiency obtained by the mass dissemination of literacy
skills far outweigh the risks posed by the possibility of un-
sanctioned mass organization. In nineteenth-century England, the Chartist movement demonstrates both the risks
and the benefits. Chartism, the working-class movement of
the early Victorian era that petitioned for such basic electoral
reforms as the secret ballot and universal male suffrage, depended on the extension of literacy skills for its cohesion, if
not its ideas. Men did not have to know how to read or write
to ask for the ballot, but these habits did make it possible for

them to organize a broad national movement that circulated published lists of demands and announced concerted campaigns for new legislation. The climax of the Chartist agitation, the "monster petition" of 1848, addressed to Parliament, was fittingly a written document subscribed by the individual signatures of a large portion of the English working class. Just as fittingly, perhaps, the Parliament laughed the petition to scorn when they discovered that many signatures were ridiculous frauds. Queen Victoria and Mr. Punch had both subscribed. Reading and writing had allowed the Chartists to publish and organize, but they could not handle language itself in the manner understood and approved by those they petitioned. They did not participate in the literacy of power and this fact helped to undermine them. Reading and writing facilitate organization, but they are no substitute for training in interpretation and the authorized uses of language.

What is more, a case could be made that the dissemination of basic literacy habits—by the time of the Chartist petition, some two-thirds of all Englishmen could read and write—actually helped to stifle instead of foment working-class agitation. Though they did not succeed in obtaining their demands, the Chartists nevertheless sensed that through their activity they had accomplished something of value. Something had been done for them and by them. While the quality of their literacy was not sufficient to alter events directly by the use of language, it was enough to mitigate the sense of resentment that grows out of frustrated incapacity to act. The great proletarian revolutions of our century—the Russian and the Chinese—have been accomplished where the working classes have had extremely low rates of reading and writing skills and consequently no means of quick and efficient organization. In the short run, their lack of organization was a boon to their masters; in the long run, it meant pent-up hostility and social upheaval. The wise tyrant would be sure to train his subjects to read and write and would even allow them the opportunity to publish their frustrations and organize their dissidence. So far he could go in relative safety. But he would also be certain that his subjects had no training in the use of the language of law or ideas. He would regulate their educations so that they learned the mechanics of language without appreciating its problems, its foundations, its subtleties, or its powers. Had the Russian royal family understood these nuances of literacy, the tsar might today be as securely entrenched in the Hermitage as the politboro is at the Kremlin.

THE CULT OF CORRECT USAGE

In twentieth-century Britain and America the kind of literacy sponsored by Locke and the nineteenth-century liberals still prevails but has evolved in often bizarre fashion. The most curious symptom of this evolution is the appearance of a school of popular critics—Edwin Newman, John Simon, and William Safire foremost among them—who champion a modern doctrine of correct usage. Let me illustrate the present condition of Locke's literacy with a story about "hopefully."

A great Midwestern university has an extension campus in a once-prosperous industrial city now gone to seed. Monolithic auto plants, many now idle because of obsolete equipment and Japanese competition, ring the old downtown area, where the university is situated among vacant lots and bus-depot vistas. The university thrives on unemployment. When the young cannot work, they go to college. Recently the university has done good business.

Among the English teachers on this urban campus is a scholar, past middle age but still vigorous. He was once an expert in the works of a renowned nineteenth-century poet, but life in the industrial heartland has curbed his appetite as well as his resources for scholarship. He remains a gentleman, however, and dresses impeccably to meet his denim-clad classes of freshman, for, like all his colleagues, he teaches each term at least one section of freshman English.

Teaching, however, has long since ceased to be the heart of the professor's life. His obsession is abuses of correct English, and chief among those he abominates is the misapplication of "hopefully." Hardly a day passes that he does not receive an offensive memo from some benighted administrator: "Hopefully, fall enrollment will be up 8 percent." "If we all pull together, hopefully the parking problem will be licked this year." Hardly a day passes that the professor does not dispatch an admonitory memo of his own denouncing the decadent English of colleagues, deans, and citizens in the world beyond—journalists, politicians, and businessmen—who seem determined to dismantle the rules of standard usage.

The professor's classes have by now grown used to his diatribes against "hopefully." These predictable digressions are for them a respite from the somniferous routine of grammar. In them the professor demonstrates flashes of eccentric passion. Hopefully, the students think, these digressions will continue.

Only someone blind to the realities of life in our century could argue that the preservation of hopefully in its eighteenth-century usage is connected in a positive way with the welfare of the professor's Midwestern students, whose fortunes are intimately related to the destiny of our beleaguered industrial economy. The story of the professor is a parable of the way an almost neurotic anxiety about the maintenance of certain linguistic rules and forms has obscured the important issues of literacy that challenge us as an economic power and as a humane society. What benefit do the professor's students derive from indoctrination in the approved use of "hopefully"? Will they earn more money in the factories by avoiding this solecism? Will they thereby qualify for better-paid executive positions? Will their personal lives be

enriched? Does the arcane knowledge of correct usage somehow elevate their spiritual beings to otherwise unapproach-
able heights? Like thousands of other words, "hopefully" has
come to have new usages. Why resist the evolution of the
language?

The mania to preserve obsolete forms of English that do
not enhance the efficiency or power of modern usage has no
economic or social benefit to the population at large. The
presence of this mania in a society that faces language problems of the first magnitude would be comic if its effects were
not so damaging. The prevailing doctrine of correct English
inhibits us from dealing with the important problems that
confront us as a literate society: some can't read or write,
others can't speak English, and few can think. The solicitude
of Simon, Newman, et al. for correct usage is reminiscent of
the anxiety of mothers who caution their daughters to wear
clean underwear in case they should be run over and un-
dressed in the emergency room. When calamity comes, say
the correctness junkies, let us meet it with propriety.

Simon and his colleagues defend their obsession with
grammatical rules and restrictive definitions by various
pleas to social justice and economic necessity. Simon quotes
the critic E. D. Hirsch with approval: "Without a normative
grapholect"—will "normative grapholect" be normative in
the new grapholect?—"Without a normative grapholect, a
classless society could not be plausibly imagined." Hirsch
only means that in a class-free world everyone would at a
minimum have to agree to use one standard of written expression. I am not sure that a class-free society would have
to do this much, but Simon goes much farther than Hirsch.
Simon uses this quotation to imply that, in a truly democratic
America, all men would at a minimum write the same brand
of English and that the only conceivable brand of English
available for this role is correct, middle-class English as practiced by John Simon. To rise to the classless bliss of the fu-

ture, the poor, the immigrant, the Southern, the Midwestern, the black must forsake dialect and learn the language of the educated, preferably Northeastern middle-class. The American revolution reaches its climax as all citizens accept a normative grapholect as propagated by Big Brother and taught by Our Miss Brooks.

Simon's classless society would be purchased at the cost of diversity and pluralism. The totalitarian rapacity of his bourgeois dream is only thinly disguised by his pretended zeal for social equality. But the social justification of correct usage does not occupy much space in any of the writings of popular linguistics. Their real concerns are elsewhere. Simon, Newman, and Safire are not harmless romantics pontificating over humorous vagaries of language. They are social critics peddling a distinct though unarticulated political ideology under the guise of popular linguistic commentary. Their ideology, not their semantics, is responsible for their large and devoted following among the American middle classes.

The mania for the preservation of standard English has its roots in the discovery by the English middle classes that a clear, concise and universal standard of language promotes what Locke called "truth," and that with "truth" comes economic prosperity, trade, industry, and bourgeois government. Locke gave this discovery its classic formulation in the seventeenth century. In the eighteenth and nineteenth centuries his philosophical descendants, the utilitarians, the radicals, and the liberals, fully exploited Locke's insight. But for Locke the correct use of language was not an ethical or even an aesthetic imperative, as it has become with Simon and his school. Correct usage was only good sense:

> To require that men should use their words constantly in the same sense, and for none but determined and uniform ideas, would be to think that all men should have the same notions, and should talk of nothing but what they have clear and distinct ideas of: which is not to be ex-

pected by anyone who hath not vanity enough to imagine
he can prevail with men to be very knowing or very silent.
. . . But though the market and exchange must be left to
their own ways of talking, and gossipings not to be robbed
of their ancient privilege: though the schools, and men of
argument would perhaps take it amiss to have anything
offered, to abate the length or lessen the number of their
disputes; yet methinks those who pretend seriously to
search after or maintain truth, should think themselves
obliged to study how they might deliver themselves without obscurity, doubtfulness, or equivocation, to which
men's words are naturally liable, if care be not taken.

Locke, unlike his dogmatic descendants, sees that correct
usage cannot be universally applied. The school and the
marketplace have their own languages, and, what is more,
no two minds can agree absolutely on the words of everyday
speech, much less conceive uniform expressions, which would
have to proceed from identical ideas. Locke sees that universal correct usage could only be accomplished by a race of
robots, or by a race of men so stripped of character as to be
almost robots. He advocates a clear and concise standard
language for limited ends: for precision in philosophical discussion and for results in practical matters where language
can be measured against realities. Philosophers can perhaps
agree on a universal definition of "essence" even if the term
applies to nothing whatever. Engineers can probably agree
on a universal definition of torque and thereby facilitate industrialism. The truth Locke discusses is both sublime and
mundane, but it was never meant by him to coerce all members of society to speak or write in one way.

Between Locke's day and our own, the notion of correct
usage has undergone a sea change. The term no longer con-
notes clear communication for philosophical or practical
advantage. Correct usage has come to be associated with all
the advantages acquired by the middle-class revolution of
the last three hundred years. This revolution was certainly

facilitated by commonly practiced linguistic norms, and we can hardly be surprised that the standards of language that helped the middle classes to power should now be enveloped in an almost mystical aura of sanctity. Correct usage was useful to the rising middle classes, and in retrospect we can understand why generations of the bourgeoisie were anxious to speak and write the purest Johnsonian English: their survival depended in part on it. But in time the connection between correct usage and practical advantage became obscure, and, as it was forgotten, the cult of correct usage began to acquire its modern characteristics: rigidity, intolerance, and lack of practical application. House dogs that sleep on soft rugs often perform an instinctive ritual. They march in a circle to mat down the straw that ceased to be part of their lives centuries ago. So the middle classes maintain a reflex worship of correct usage.

The conjunction of standard English and middle-class ideology was already firmly established in the nineteenth century. In *Cranford*, her 1853 portrait of domestic life in an early nineteenth-century English village, Mrs. Gaskell gives us a portrait of the cult of correct usage in the character of Miss Jenkyns, the incarnation of middle-class gentility, who idolizes Dr. Johnson and believes that the young Charles Dickens might make something of himself "if he will take the great Doctor for his model." Miss Jenkyns's linguistic preferences support the social conventions and amenities she holds most dear, as well as the regular interest payments that finance her gentility. Thackeray, approaching the same subject from a different perspective in *Vanity Fair*, has Becky Sharp chuck Dr. Johnson's dictionary out of a coach window as she leaves school and sets out for London. Her abuse of the great Doctor is an emblem of her coming assault not merely on the proprieties of correct usage, but on the whole social order of the Regency period.

In *Vanity Fair* Becky Sharp is crushed by the conventions she flouts. It was Cranford with its social and linguistic conventions that triumphed as the model of civilized life in the nineteenth century. Cranford lives on in the works of Newman and company. Even as objective and thoughtful a critic as George Steiner succumbs to middle-class nostalgia when he concludes a brilliant study of the fortunes of modern English with the wistful observation that "the externals of English are being acquired by speakers wholly alien to the historical fabric, to the inventory of felt moral, cultural existence embedded in the language."

Correct usage no longer has the pragmatic sense it did in Locke's day. It now signifies genteel conformity to a rigid set of codes, some written, some tacit. The written codes of correct usage include the standard English grammars and style books. The tacit rules of language are usually those conventions of middle-class Anglo-American usage that have come to have aesthetic value to their users. Correct usage has two dimensions, prescriptive and aesthetic. Do these two have any historical or practical validity? Why are sections of our society so concerned that correct usage be maintained?

The prescriptive approach to language is represented by what grammarians, followed by John Simon, have touted as the rules of grammar and sought to give the force of immutable law. This has most commonly been done by promulgating rules for English grammar by analogy with Latin. But these rules have no God-given validity. They merely reflect the distilled practice of centuries of English users and more centuries of Latin users before them. And, in any case, the analogy with Latin, so dear to the hearts of prescriptive grammarians, cuts two ways. Latin grammarians had frequently to make exceptions to the rules of good Latin usage when they encountered apparent anomalies in the works of the best classical authors. Indeed, good Latin grammars consist largely of a series of exceptions. Surely good English, if it is to be structured like good classical writing, ought to be allowed the same exceptions. For instance, in the sentence "The whole cellful of prisoners, all of whom have long since exhausted their appeals, are scheduled to be executed at dawn tomorrow," the verb ought, strictly speaking, to be singular. According to Latin grammar, however, the plural is permitted by exception.

At its best, grammar is descriptive and redeems us from the intolerance of blanket prescriptions. On the Latin model many of the outrages of popular speech and writing against which the Simons and Newmans fulminate cannot only be described but justified. The textbook example of a dangling participle, "Being a nice day, he went for a walk," is after all only an English version of the Latin ablative. In this example, the so-called error produces no loss of sense or clarity. Anyone might make the mistake, but only an idiot could misunderstand it. Why is it wrong? A precedent can be cited even for the vulgar term of approbation "dyno-fuckin'-mite!"—a rare English example of the classical rhetorical device tmesis, the splitting of one word to allow another word in its midst. Surely a device used by Vergil and bearing an imposing classical pedigree cannot be vulgar. Prescriptive grammar can usually be defeated by appealing to its own traditions. Lacking real historical validity, prescriptive grammar relies on rant and intimidation to achieve its authority.

The prescriptive rules of modern grammar illustrate the fortunes of literacy in the last two hundred years. The eighteenth century advocated clarity of communication as a means toward a materially rewarding "truth." The original rule, then, was not grammar for its own sake but grammar as one means toward comprehension. In our day the means has become more important than the end. Rules are enforced on a population of readers and writers who now strive not to make their language clear and profitable but socially acceptable according to the middle-class standards of the past. Prescriptive grammar in our day is nostalgia as repression.

Finally, however, the champions of standard English have a higher aim than promulgating prescriptive laws of language. They seek to preserve the beauty or spirit of the language. The coda of John Simon's tirade, *Paradigms Lost,* makes the aesthetic of standard English clear: "The time must be at hand when we shall hear—not just 'Don't ask for who the bell rings' (*ask not* and *tolls* being, of course, archaic, elitist language), but also 'It rings for you and I'!" According to the cult of correct usage, once we forsake the old standards, we will have lost our capacity to create beauty in language. In this view, the longing of the human spirit finds its most glorious expression in the formal language of the English Renaissance.

Simon is at least half right. As English changes in response to popular pressures—as *tolls* passes out of everyday speech and as *whom* is universally subdued to *who* in the progressive abolition of declensions in English over more than a thousand years—the possibility of our culture's producing another Donne falls to zero. No one will ever again write Donne's sublime *Devotions on Emergent Occasions,* but Frank O'Hara could write the beautiful jazz poetry of *Meditations in an Emergency.* No one will ever again create a Shakespearean play or a Miltonic epic, but it does not follow that the English language will never again produce works of beauty or spiritual richness. Aesthetic taste changes with language, and the glories of contemporary English will be set to the popular language that Simon despises. The prose of Burroughs or Beckett, the lyric of Ashbery or David Byrne, are not beautiful by the standards of eighteenth-century English, but they inspire reverence in larger audiences than ever Dr. Johnson reached in his life. The aesthetic has changed to conform to the change in our language.

We have come far enough to see Simon and company in a clearer light. Their prescriptions for English are not primarily intended to improve clarity or utility or social equality. They are rules designed to perpetuate the aesthetic and the ideology behind English usage in Britain and America from the 1600s through the opening decades of this century. History shows the political nature of grammar and lexicography. In the sardonic columns of Simon and his cohorts we can see the reactionary character of the cult of correct usage. In the eighteenth century theirs was the party of progress, the party of the rising middle classes that with Locke advocated a standard language as a means to truth, and, more than truth, profit. In our century the victory of this party is complete. Advocacy of standard English is no longer a revolutionary phenomenon but a means of perpetuating the language and the ideas of the triumphant middle classes.

The champions of correct usage are in part responsible for some of the abuses of language that they condemn. No one can enjoy reading or writing English full of false Latin coinages, twisted euphemisms, and pompous elocutions. Edwin Newman complains that he receives letters with phrases like "penetration of significant audience strata" in them from colleagues who mean to say "important people watched our show." He denounces these excesses at some length, but he and his counterparts in the cult of correct usage are largely responsible for creating them. The overblown language of modern business is a misguided attempt by its practitioners to imitate the formal grandeur that the advocates of correct English have falsely proclaimed to be the essence of good usage. The deluded businessman who asks a client to finalize a transaction aspires to be something better than a plain-spoken man of the streets. He wants to imitate the language of the dominant classes, and he believes he does this by language that elevates his prose. The pompous use of English is a symptom that in popular thought the relation between clarity, common sense, and good usage has disappeared. For the social climber, the model of proper usage is bombast produced according to intricate rules understood only by the initiate. Under the leadership of Simon and company correct usage bears the same relation to eighteenth-century English that Baptist snake-handling cults bear to early Christianity.

SOME THOUGHTS ON TEACHING ENGLISH

If the notion of standard English has been debased in our day, what should we teach students in school? Should they learn to read and write without rules? Not if they hope to succeed in the American economy. The norms of correct usage may be false, pretentious, and outdated, but they are the standards of literate behavior demanded in government, business, and the professions. Students who want to get ahead in American civilization must continue to learn standard English for its social utility—not, as its champions would have them believe, its moral necessity. Even the sanctimonious brand of correct English peddled in the American educational establishment has the advantage of providing a single form of profitable communication. We would lose this single standard only at great cost to our material well-being.

What the educational system needs is not a change of curriculum but a change of attitude. Students who come to the classroom speaking and writing a variety of dialects, jargons, and grammars are understandably repelled when informed that their native habits of language are wrong and unbeautiful. Surely it is possible to teach the necessity of standard English without accusing a pupil of stupidity. But the shrill tone of the champions of correct usage insists upon the virtue of the norm and therefore the depravity of those who deviate from it.

One student writes about a movie called *The Incredible Melting Man* that "the hero of the movie is a doctor if you can call him a hero. His actions are so foolish that he gets himself killed over a melting man whose dying anyway. All in all, the movie sucks, and the special effect don't make it any tighter of a movie. So unless your in for a horror movie that makes you laugh, your better off spending your money on a case of beer and watching the tube at home." In the normal course of events, this student can expect to watch his prose disintegrate into a red porridge of corrections about tone, diction, punctuation, and the distinction between who's and whose, you're and your. From repeated doses of correction he certainly will not learn to write. Instead he will lose all confidence in himself as a user of English. He will simply stop committing his best thought and vital interest to words, words framed, that is, in the approved fashion.

This process of alienation explains in part why the average college freshman has so little to say on paper. As a result of the middle-class norm of correct usage, standard English has become an intimidating, humiliating medium that stifles expression. Many teachers promulgate the rules of standard English not as conveniences but as imperatives. Many others, disgusted with the prescriptions of correct usage, encourage their students to indulge their feelings and emotions with slight regard for forms of linguistic discipline. Caught between intimidating rigidity and brainless license, it is no wonder that young Americans have given up on the socially approved variety of literacy as a means of expressing their vitality. The young have developed a language of their own, unhampered by traditional linguistic authority. The next chapter looks at this phenomenon more closely. Here I only want to make a few general observations about the present realities of English and how these can best be met in the classroom.

"I avoid English classes as though it were some contagious disease, this is probably do in part to my fear of failure," writes a freshman. "Lack of agreement, comma splice, spelling error," comes the professorial reply to this intelligent self-diagnosis. Yet none of the errors committed in this example or the earlier *Melting Man* critique, is fatal to comprehension, and the level of intelligence in both quotations is respectable. Like most young Americans, these authors have a different set of spelling and grammatical notions that, if practiced consistently, make as much sense as those used by John Simon. The students differ from Simon in being unconscious of the forms they use or any alternatives to them, but the great majority of writers are unconscious most of the time of the conventions within which they work. Is the role of the English teacher to exact mechanical adherence to an established set of linguistic standards or to develop the consciousness of language necessary for the student to comprehend his own linguistic conventions?

The answer, I think, is that the teacher must in justice do both. And so I have three general suggestions about teaching English.

First, standard English should be taught as a practical tool of social advantage, never as a moral or aesthetic norm. Even the so-called illiterate students abused in the popular press are acute enough to understand the logic behind learning established forms for economic survival. On the other hand, the logic that presents correct English as an ethical necessity is false, and students rightly reject it. With the false logic, they wrongly reject the language they need to learn. We need an honest rationale for teaching standard English.

Second, standard English should be treated as a second language, not as the correct form of the language the student already speaks and writes. In many cases, formal English *is* a second language for students. It has many points of similarity with vernacular English, but is nonetheless a radically different level of language. Formal English should be taught from an early age in much the same way Latin used to be taught. Students should not be made to feel inadequate because the language of their daily lives and feelings does not correspond with the formal language of our society, but they should be required to learn the rules and uses of this formal language for their own economic good. The goal of teaching formal English as a second language should be to provide all citizens with the ability to read and write all those public documents by which society organizes itself.

Third, students should be encouraged to think, speak, and write according to their own conceptions of literacy. Teachers should permit the greatest possible freedom in students' personal writing, with these understandings: that society at large will not accept ideas written in this form; that the speech and writing must be clear and comprehensible according to its own standards; that the student should develop his awareness of the uses of language as a result of his own writing.

Students ought to be allowed to find their own voice without being buried beneath a melancholy heap of rhetorics, style-sheets, and how-to-write manifestos. "I feel that if all the information is there why be concerned with general to specific and upside down triangles," writes one freshman. Good question, even without a question mark.

I can see no harm in students' possessing more than one form of English. In fact, if they are taught formal English in a pragmatic vein, they may absorb some of the terminology and grammar necessary for them to understand the forms at work in their own very different prose. At present, terminology and grammar are taught in such a haphazard, condescending, and intimidating way that they are not learned at all.

I am recommending that we admit, as the medieval world did in the Carolingian reforms of 813, that we have two languages, an official and a vernacular. I think we must face the reality that no one will again speak or write vitally in the language of Shakespeare or Cromwell or Lincoln or even William Jennings Bryan. People will, however, speak and write with spirit and intelligence in new forms of language presently coming to life, and we should give these new forms their freedom. At the same time we must preserve the economic and social benefits that arise from a formal language like correct English, This we must do by ensuring that all citizens not only know the formal language well enough to use it in social life but also clearly understand the practical rationale behind their training in it.

I do not believe these recommendations would lead us into a dark age. The two literacies of the Middle Ages were oppressive because only a few had access to the literacy of power. The essence of my suggestion is that all citizens should have access to the language of power. As presently taught, English alienates the already disadvantaged from the chief vehicle of self-knowledge and social order—language. Bewildered by the norms of formal English and oblivious of their own literacy, the young and the poor still wait to be taught a language of life, not a regimen of liberal nostalgia.

CHAPTER SEVEN

Caliban in America: Literacy in the Age of Rock

By the time of the American Revolution, the number of adult males in the New England colonies who could read and write approached 90 percent of the population. The best study of reading and writing skills in New England attributes the development and dissemination of these talents to the pervasive influence of Protestantism. Protestantism invited first-hand acquaintance with sacred texts. In addition, the Protestant ethic encouraged social mobility and trade, which in turn stimulated the market for reading and writing. The figures for reading and writing skills in colonial New England were almost certainly higher than the comparable rates in the Southern colonies, but there too the mechanical skills of literacy were widespread, more so than is generally believed.

The religious ethic of the colonists made them simultaneously readers and bourgeois revolutionaries. They read to interpret. Their reading was both a symptom of and an incentive to their critical spirit. It promoted their capacity for social organization while abetting their zealous pragmatism, the result of a combination of Bunyan's and Locke's kinds of literacy. The Yankee literate brought to the New World Bunyan's faith that the Word speaks directly to the ready soul, but he also exploited Locke's notion that the uses of the Word manifest themselves in practical, social gains. Because of his literacy, the eighteenth-century American could and did claim to stand on the threshold of a new world order, the *novus ordo seclorum*. He was in many respects, especially in his literacy, the prototypical modern man.

But times change, and nothing more poignantly illustrates that literacy is a relative and evolving aspect of cultural life than the comparison of early American literacy with its off-spring in contemporary society. The descendant of the colonial American literate is today's member of the Moral Majority. His book is also the Bible. He too is a hard-working member of the bourgeoisie. I doubt, however, that we could expect this descendant of the early American literates to generate anew the new order of the ages. In fact, he is often regarded as a throwback or called an illiterate, even though he is motivated by the same enthusiasms and equipped with the same skills as those early Americans we consider the progenitors of our liberty. Since the eighteenth century, America has evolved a new form of literacy, descended from the literacy of the colonial period but altered by new attitudes and new technologies.

MECHANICAL LITERACY

What distinguishes literacy in late twentieth-century America from literacy here in the colonial period is not superior mechanical ability. Boston probably had about the same proportion of skilled readers and writers in the eighteenth century that it does today, and if we apply the standard of so-called functional literacy to the towns of Virginia in Jefferson's time and those of contemporary Virginia, it may be that as large a percentage of the population then could use literacy skills in a practical way as can now. I mention these possibilities not to humiliate the present. America began with a high rate of reading and writing skills throughout its population, and it has maintained or improved on that level.

What does distinguish today's literacy in America from literacy here two hundred years ago is that we now approach the subject with anxiety while our ancestors invested it with their accustomed optimism. The most telling fact about literacy in modern America is not declining Scholastic Aptitude Test scores or the advent of electronic media or welfare applicants who cannot fill out bureaucratic forms or junior executives who cannot punctuate. The most telling fact is the profusion of concern, expressed in a seemingly endless stream of books, symposia, newspaper columns, and television talk shows, that literacy in America has failed in some essential way, imperiling our survival as a culture.

Among the most commonly cited causes for this alleged failure of literacy in America today is the low level of functional reading and writing skills among the general population, prominent among the poor but insidiously gaining within the ranks of the white middle class. Commentators quote Jefferson's remark that "if a nation expects to be ignorant and free in a state of civilization, it expects what never was and never will be." They point out that the shoddy state of reading and writing skills among the American young endangers our way of life. "We jeopardize our freedom if we do not make every attempt to teach all of our citizens the knowledge they need to make the good choices that will keep our democracy operating," warns a typical critic.

The argument that the survival of American civilization rests upon the universal dissemination of reading and writing skills has prompted a return to basics in elementary, secondary, and higher education. Teach each child to read and write efficiently, and he will become a citizen capable of making the good choices necessary for democratic government.

This argument and its practical manifestations in our educational system rest on the fallacious logic of Mill's liberalism. Liberalism argues that by teaching a man to read and write, you also teach him to think. The experience of past centuries suggests, as we have seen, that this premise is not true. It would be more correct to say that by teaching a man to read and write, you teach him to read and write. He has learned mechanical skills, but the acquisition of the skills in itself gives him no special insight into the creative or advantageous use of these skills. Even Jefferson, who is too often quoted as the champion of the flawed logic of the liberal position, clearly realized the distinction between the mechanical skills of literacy and the added power to employ them creatively. In his *Notes on the State of Virginia* he envisioned an educational system where the dullards are weeded out early and only those students who demonstrate an aptitude for the imaginative manipulation of basic skills are trained further. "By this means twenty of the best geniuses will be raked from the rubbish annually, and be instructed, at public expense, so far as the grammar schools go. . . . The ultimate result of the whole scheme of education would be the teaching all the children of the State reading, writing, and common arithmetic, turning out ten annually of superior genius well taught in Greek, Latin, geography and the higher branches of arithmetic." Under Jefferson's educational scheme, the masses would be versed in the mechanics of reading and writing, but there is no illusion that the "rubbish" would thereby become a rational citizenry.

Why, then, bother to teach reading and writing at all if they do not in themselves make citizens better? The answer is inherent in the structure of literacy programs everywhere and especially in the organization of functional literacy drives in America. These programs concentrate on the formation of those reading and writing skills necessary for the transfer of basic information within the society. They seek to ensure that workers will be able to read operating instructions, fill out job applications, and submit financial information on the requisite government forms. A favorite test of so-called functional literacy is whether the testee can read a newspaper well enough to find the help-wanted ads most appropriate to his training or the supermarket sales that provide him with the most economical meals. When we in America give a man the tools of reading and writing, we expect him to become more efficient, not more intelligent. Mechanical skill with the technologies of reading and writing is essential for America, but not because it inculcates democratic habits or creates a judicious population. Reading and writing skills by themselves, it is thought, promote social cohesion and efficiency. They are necessary for productivity. The citizen who cannot read or write is an economic liability to himself and his society.

Literacy tests in our society stress the transfer of information, not thought. In fact, Americans have come to equate testing for interpretive competency with bigotry. The literacy tests for voters applied against Southern blacks asked not for mere mechanical skill in reading and writing but for critical ability as well. "Every elector shall . . . be able to read any section of the Constitution of this state or he shall be able to understand the same when read to him, or give a reasonable interpretation thereof." This is the language of the Mississippi State Constitution of 1892. The citizen here need not even be asked to read. He may pass the test by "a reasonable interpretation." Such tests are repugnant to the democratic spirit for several reasons. They are subjective in their determination of what is "reasonable." They may be applied selectively. But, further, they make a demand on the citizen body which is not included in the American people's list of necessary social attainments: the ability to reason and interpret.

The popular prejudice against critical competency tests for admission to the privileges of citizenship is well founded. Whether he reasons or interprets in any trained way, a man is still part of the social fabric and ought to be allowed to express his feelings with the ballot. We ought, however, to be suspicious of the contention that a man who reads and writes does in fact make an informed choice in the performance of his various social duties. Intentionally or not, the result of mass literacy in industrial America as elsewhere has been to train the citizen body only for social efficiency and obedience. A study published in 1977 by the Department of Health, Education and Welfare describes the state of literacy among American seventeen-year-olds in 1974. It found that 90 percent of seventeen-year-olds could read and describe a job ad in the newspaper; 85 percent could read a map; 78 percent could read an index; 75 percent could fathom the phone company's instructions for dialing long-distance; and an astounding 60 percent could understand the phone company's long-distance rate charts. A concerned citizen would naturally hope these figures might all approach 100 percent, but, while they are not ideal, they are nonetheless good. They reveal a highly organized populace, the great majority of whom are well versed in comprehending the information necessary for the efficient transaction of business within a technological economy. Smaller, more homogeneous economies like those of Great Britain and the Scandinavian countries have achieved greater mechanical proficiency among their populations, but considering the size, history, and diversity of America, the level of efficient communication through reading and writing skills is high. It is also essential to our economic survival that citizens should be able effectively to find their way in the job markets and to carry out the written or printed directives by which an advanced society lives.

Attainment of the mechanics of literacy, however, has little bearing upon the ability of citizens to understand or interpret complex ideas, as the HEW study shows. Between 50 and 60 percent of the seventeen-year-olds tested understood a brief passage describing the function of the Supreme Court. This was the highest percentage of correct response to any interpretive question in the test, and, typically, the correct reply involves comprehension not so much of a thought as of a social mechanism. From this point onward, critical skills declined, both in reading and writing. "From one-third to one-half of the students were able to identify the author's intent or the main idea after reading passages selected from articles or textbooks likely to be read by college freshmen." Asked to write an essay using as a point of departure the situation shown in a picture, the students' average paper was 137 words long (the HEW study fondly calls this a "long essay"), their average word, four letters long. Ten percent of these long essays were "carefully developed papers with definite moods and made no serious errors in composition." Asked to respond in writing to a poem called "The Closing of the Rodeo"—a typically bogus assignment—about one-half gave brief evaluative comments ("It was good"), and one-third noted some trivial aspect of the poem ("It rhymes"). Many gave brief expressions of feelings ("I don't like cowboys"). The study concludes with laconic pathos: "Seventeen-year-olds cannot write well in an unstructured, nondirective situation."

And why should they? The function of training in the mechanics of literacy is not—cannot be—to develop the critical mind. This project would require another kind of training not generally available in the American scheme of education. Much of the current concern about literacy in America grows out of a mistaken belief that mechanical literacy ought to complement the acquisition of certain rational skills that make the good citizen, but the fact is that the mechanical habits of reading and writing are not sufficient for the development of the critical mind. Many students instinctively realize that the mechanics of literacy have nothing to do with the larger cultural advancements expected of them. "Writing courses in college should teach the student how to write a business letter and resumes, with minimal gramatical errors," says one freshman essay. "It can never hurt anyone to write a critical essay, it will only make that person seem more cultured, but considering the fact that the average student only attends about seventy-two hours of english classes in his four years of college, there is very little time to write." This sentiment, presented in the sort of language over which teachers shake their heads in sadness, nonetheless represents a valid argument. Critical thought might make a person seem more cultured, but in the short amount of time the system has to turn out functional members of an industrial economy, this student believes that the emphasis ought to be on the practical mechanics of language that lead to the correct and efficient production of résumés and business letters. The student's essay reveals that the system has failed to achieve even this modest goal, but he wants nothing more than to be taught enough of the mechanics of literacy to enable him to make a good living in the highly developed economy of his country. He is not unique.

Consider the alternative: a world in which the young are uniformly trained not merely in the mechanics of reading and writing, but in some critical attitude toward language necessary as a first step in the formation of literacy. This kind of educational endeavor has been the dream of visionaries from Plato to Lenin, and, as Lenin observed, it would produce not merely the functional skills requisite to the successful exploitation of a modern economy but the critical insight necessary for popular opposition to stifling institutions and oppressive ideologies. I am assuming, with abandoned idealism, that such an educational program could be carried out with a minimum of political bias, so that students would not merely be brainwashed in a particular social creed, as they are by literacy campaigns, but would in fact be taught critical habits of language applicable universally and impartially.

Stating the alternative makes it clear why this kind of literacy does not exist, why it is not likely soon to exist. None of our institutions desires it; very few citizens are eager for it. The probable first act of a population that had the universal capability of discoursing with critical acumen on the poem "The Closing of the Rodeo" would be to abolish the system that used "The Closing of the Rodeo" as an educational text. The same logic applies throughout the institutions of established power. They have an investment in the propagation of the mechanics of literacy and an equal investment in the restriction of any broader training in critical consciousness of language. Viewed in this light, the current state of literacy in America, far from being the unwanted disaster it is often advertised to be, is the state of events desired by the prevailing institutions.

FOLLOWERS AND LEADERS: TWO LITERACIES

If those who control the ruling institutions have no wish to face a populace well trained in the dynamics of language and thought, neither does the populace itself want to be so trained. Like the student who has nothing against culture but prefers to learn how to write a résumé, the majority of the population would like to learn those practical aspects of literacy clearly connected with the attainment of realistic employment and with career advancement.

In our society, those who have reading and writing skills achieve a minimal level of social usefulness, as well as a sense of belonging. The construction worker recorded by Ann Landers who burst into tears when his wife discovered he was unable to read or write was mortified not by his intellectual defects or by any economic hardship—he made a good living—but by his social isolation in a world of other men who shared the mechanical talents of literacy. The present anxiety about the state of literacy in America is directed largely toward the failure to make the mechanical skills of reading and writing universal. This anxiety is well founded. A modern state that does not achieve universal mechanical skills of this sort may be visited with several social evils. Most obviously, it will lose in the rapid transfer of commands and social information. The presence in the midst of our society of a large group of people who because of a lack of basic skills cannot respond to written information imperils the existing order of society just as certainly as if the same group consciously chose to disobey or ignore this information. The final result is the same: a failure of social obedience.

These non-readers and non-writers further threaten the cultural fabric because they lack the sense of community and equality fostered by the spread of mechanical literacy. A study that professes to show that some blacks now affect illiteracy as a badge of social distinction is evidence of the danger society runs by permitting some of its members to be deficient in the basic skills of literacy. If it is true, as some studies suggest, that the number of Americans who cannot intelligibly deal with the basic printed documents of our civilization approaches something like 40 percent of the population, the potential for social discord might seem to be proportionately as great. These figures are misleading, however, because by the very nature of their disadvantage mechanical illiterates are for the most part incapable of effective, coordinated social protest, a phenomenon that in our society requires basic reading and writing skills and perhaps some higher forms of thought as well. But because this illiterate lumpenproletariat is disorganized, it is also volatile and unpredictable. It may flash with anger in the streets or in the voting booth, for while mechanical illiterates cannot read or write, they can vote.

The revolutionary menace posed by non-readers and non-writers is, however, easily exaggerated. Tests for functional illiteracy overrate the problem by using as a standard of literacy competence in the use of government forms that by their nature are confusing. Bureaucracies stay in business by proliferating forms that generate a need for still more bureaucrats. Even professors have difficulty understanding a tax or unemployment form. Functional literacy tests also tacitly assume that the poor are illiterate and then seek to prove this hidden thesis by the nature of their questions. Thus these tests concentrate heavily on the respondents' capacity to fathom criminal law, welfare regulations, and other bewildering areas of social policy that are thorny questions to most citizens, including Supreme Court justices.

The gravity of our literacy problem may have been exaggerated not only because of the biased nature of the test results we have but because most so-called illiterates, like the weeping construction worker, would prefer to be inside rather than outside the community of readers and writers. As long as these illiterates aspire to conform, they will represent an economic liability but not a revolutionary threat.

On the whole, given its size, diverse population, and heritage, America has indeed done well in the spread of reading and writing skills. That the great majority of Americans speak English, is admirable, and that they can read and write it is more so. That at least 85 percent of seventeen-year-old high-school students can read classified ads and maps gives us the basis of a coherent and efficient industrial machine. The present concern over the state of basic literacy skills is itself a cause for optimism despite the anxiety that needlessly afflicts our culture as it contemplates the subject. Americans seem determined to spread the habits of reading and writing throughout the entire population, and this commitment is evidence of a desire for improved social organization and economic efficiency. Though this undertaking will take time, even to start is a success of sorts.

TRAINING THE LITERATE ELITE

Literacy is an ambiguous word in our society. On the one hand it implies a rational application of the mind to the problems of language, an exalted cultural achievement. On the other it means the acquisition of mechanical skills in reading and writing, an important but not usually noble attainment. The ambiguity of the term allows for a pretense of egalitarianism in our culture while in fact we maintain a highly structured social hierarchy. Almost all Americans can read and write. Thus we seem to be equal. But very few Americans possess discipline in the habits of language necessary for its advantageous use, and those few who do effectively control the many who do not.

Rigorous, occasionally monomaniacal training in the uses of language is the essence of the literacy of power and is necessary for advancement to positions of authority. This requirement is not, as it may first seem, arbitrary. It is the means by which cultures ensure that their leaders are capable of scrutinizing the problems presented by language in a creative and rewarding fashion, and the problems presented through the medium of language may range from spoken and written orders to the entire structure of mental and cultural life.

The ways in which societies have chosen to teach and test the literacy necessary for power often seem bizarre, but, properly understood, they have a common purpose. The Roman ruling class was brought up on a strict educational diet of rhetoric, a tedious regimen of study that nonetheless assured the state of a leadership skilled in examining and manipulating language. The Chinese bureaucracy for many centuries tested its prospective members by asking them to write critical essays on the doctrines of Confucian thought. The medieval churchman was raised on the intellectual regimen of formal logic, and in the nineteenth century the British accepted as evidence of those qualities necessary to administer the Indian subcontinent ease in translation of Horace and Vergil and familiarity with the canon of English literature. Neither Rome, nor China, nor the Church, nor Britain was the loser by these tests, the aim of which was to select the most literate men for positions of authority.

Similar standards and tests of literacy exist in modern America as well, though they are not so highly formalized. Although we have a number of formal examinations for admission to positions of authority, such as the civil service and the bar, perhaps the single most exacting test to which aspirants to authority are subjected is the challenge of admission to and graduation from one of the colleges or universities that supply the leadership for Amercia's government, business, and professions. Attending Harvard, Stanford, or the University of Michigan is no guarantee of entry into the circles of power, but these circles are lopsidedly inhabited by graduates of these universities and their sister institutions. Since World War II admission to these universities has depended in large measure on satisfactory scores on the Scholastic Aptitude Test. This test therefore plays a central role in determining which Americans are literate enough to receive the further training that prepares them for leadership positions. In recent years, the average verbal score of all those students taking the SAT has declined, and many observers are alarmed, equating a decline in the average score with a general decline in the level of American literacy.

The Educational Testing Service, which administers the SAT, gives two reasons for the decline in test scores over the last twenty years. First, more and more students, often poorer and more poorly educated than earlier testees, have begun to take the test, and the falling scores reflect the presence of this expanding population. Second, in the last fifteen years students from all classes and backgrounds have slipped in their verbal aptitude as measured by the SAT. This second reason is the one that evokes concerned articles and worried editorials from the media.

The decline in the scores and its causes are clues to the nature and evolution of American literacy. In 1947 the SAT assumed its present form and sponsorship under the ETS. Some 81,000 high school students took it in the academic year 1951-52, out of a total eighteen-year-old population of two million, of whom some 26 percent matriculated at college. Those taking the SAT represented a small minority of the college-bound population. They were the white, middle-class high-school students trained in some aspect of the critical uses of language, whether by studying rhetoric, foreign languages, or critical analysis. These students represented that fraction of the population who went on to college in preparation for assuming leading roles in American business, government, and professional life.

By 1976-77 the number of eighteen-year-olds in the population had doubled while the number of graduating high school students taking the SAT had risen from 81,000 to 1,401,000, a seventeen-fold increase. Meanwhile the number of institutions of higher education had gone up from about 1800 in 1950 to around 3100 in 1978. Most of the additional students now in the higher education system have not been trained—or have been trained only very sloppily—in the uses of language. They are only readers and writers. Most of them cannot expect leadership roles in society. They must be content to be paid a living wage as functionaries. Most of them aspire to no more.

The SAT still directs itself toward testing those verbal skills possessed by the literate white upper middle classes of 1950. No wonder the test scores have declined. More and more students who can read and write but who have not been trained in the uses of language that mark the literacy of privilege in America have taken the test. They have increasingly dragged the mean score down. The portion of the so-called new illiteracy revealed by the test-score decline is therefore not a new phenomenon but merely indicates statistically what has always been the case—that America is divided along fairly rigid class lines and that the upper classes control the social institutions and perpetuate their control by training their young in the established habits of literacy. The lower orders learn to read and write, but they do not learn the requisite skills of language that would permit them to score high on the SAT. Meanwhile, the trained literates are passed along to the top colleges, from which the society's leadership comes.

Do these colleges perpetuate their influence by training more literate students who are therefore better suited to authority, or do they merely establish an old-boy network, by elevating their graduates to power even where equal or superior merit might be found outside the system?

American government, businesses, and professions are undeniably clubbish. I am looking at Dun and Bradstreet's *Reference Book of Corporate Management* for 1980-81. The major national corporations show a remarkably similar pattern of leadership. Here is a West Coast example. Of the eighteen top officers of TransAmerica Corporation, one of America's wealthiest and largest, four went to Stanford and the rest, one each, to Princeton, Brown, UCLA, University of Redlands, University of California at Davis, MIT, University of Washington, Dartmouth, Drexel, Boston University, Occidental, Miami University, Wayne University, and Fordham. Here top management has favored the best West Coast colleges, especially the chief executive's alma mater, Stanford. Can it be that only this select group of white middleclass males is able to administer the destinies of TransAmerica or have these gentlemen merely cloned themselves? Is their education simply a social introduction to power or is it really a means to superior literacy?

According to Lady Bird Johnson, her husband, no friend of East Coast elitism, was forced to appoint "people who were graduates of Harvard, Yale, or Princeton, or of a small nucleus of schools on the far West Coast" to cabinet posts and government agencies because they "got a better preparation at some of those schools." Here the graduates of the select universities proliferated not because of but in spite of the old-boy network. Besides aiding students to make social contacts, these universities foster the brand of literacy that has come to be nearly a prerequisite for leadership in American life. The American educational establishment teaches three distinct levels of literacy: at the select schools, like those mentioned by Lady Bird, the predominant American literacy is taught; at a large number of institutions, most opened in the last forty years, the literacy is plainly vocational; and at an even larger, nebulous body of schools professing to be liberal-arts institutions the students are given a literacy that imitates the brand of both the select colleges and of the vocational colleges without achieving the aims of either. This last group is the most problematical section of American higher education at the present moment.

The select schools that propagate the literacy sanctioned by our culture can be recognized by the numbers of their graduates in positions of influence. The *Reference Book of Corporate Managements* tells me that of the top executives at Citicorp, three each attended Harvard, Yale, and Brown, while others are graduates of Wesleyan, Georgetown, Northwestern, Fordham, Columbia, Dartmouth, Williams, and the University of Wisconsin. High-school dropouts may take comfort in the knowledge that one of the top positions at Citicorp is filled by a man who did not go to college. He is, however, British, and trained with the Royal Air Force.

The institutions that provide the manpower for American leadership are marked by a commitment to programs in languages and literature. They are the universities that still have classics departments and the colleges where English is still a popular major. Their successful graduates do not all come from language programs, but all have been trained in an atmosphere where a certain ease and facility in the critical uses of language is deemed not only important but praiseworthy. Even the good-natured jocks who graduate from these colleges collect small libraries and pay deference to skill with words—indeed, it is largely their generous financial support that funds the endowments of these institutions and endows chairs in linguistics or Latin.

The great majority of people in positions of real power in America have emerged from institutions that maintain traditional, language-oriented curricula. The hegemony of these literates continues, even thrives, in the age of software. Executives in industries that rely on new computer technologies tell me that when they want someone to run a computer center or oversee a program design, they look for humanities majors because they are adept at manipulating systems of thought and verbal patterns. In a few years most computers will be programmed to respond to ordinary English, and the day of the specialist in computer languages like BASIC will be over. What will become of those students who hoped to make their fortunes by majoring in areas of technological expertise like computer programming? They will be working for English majors from Berkeley and Harvard. *Plus ça change* . . .

Within the select institutions that supply America with its literates, literacy still means an ability to deal with language critically and profoundly. Those colleges where this attitude still prevails are the privileged ones that provide our literate leadership. They take their students from among those young people whose training has already yielded evidence of acceptable literacy, say in SAT scores, or whose record indicates that they will be amenable to the literate curriculum of the institution. I once read a diatribe by a faculty member at Columbia denouncing the spread of illiteracy across the country and into his own classroom. After several pages of fulmination, however, the reader learned that the professor considered his students illiterate because they were unversed in critical approaches to Aeschylus and Cervantes. Imagine a freshman unacquainted with the Oresteia! Meanwhile only 10 percent of seventeen-year-olds can write a competent "long essay" on "The Closing of the Rodeo."

At the other end of the spectrum, where Cervantes and Aeschylus are almost unknown, are colleges that are admittedly vocational in purpose. Among these are not only technical schools that teach a particular trade, but most junior colleges and a number of four-year colleges. In these institutions there are often large English departments, but their role is almost wholly to teach the basics of reading and writing. They teach only the mechanics of literacy and can be recognized by their low enrollments in language programs of all types. In these schools the students generally avoid any language-oriented courses except as required and favor curricula geared to getting good, practical jobs.

ILLITERATE BACKLASH

There seems to be a paradox in this system. The students who reject anything more than mechanical training in language because it is of no apparent economic benefit go on to be employed by corporations that are run by the graduates of colleges where training in language forms the heart of the curriculum. Paradoxical or not, though, the system is realistic. The students at junior colleges do not aspire to the board room of Citicorp, and, in the jobs to which they do aspire, the vocational skills they seek are probably more useful to them. This dual system of higher education is built on a tacit assumption with which the majority of the American people seem to feel comfortable, that while all citizens should know how to read and write, only those destined for positions of authority need to be literate, provided that access to the select literate curricula is not absolutely restricted to members of one class or wage bracket.

A number of American colleges, however, conform to neither of these models. In them, the students would very much like to reach positions of power in the professions, corporations, and government bodies that together form the American economy. These ambitious students want to reach positions normally held by the literate elite through what appears to them the most practical route, job-oriented courses. The prospective doctor wants biology courses, the prospective technocrat, computer courses, the prospective corporate executive, business courses. In a time of competition for students, liberal-arts colleges are quick to satisfy the growing demand for practical curricula.

The result of this pragmatic educational policy is evident in a wide range of second-rank colleges throughout the country. These schools can be recognized by their English curriculum. Freshmen first take a writing course where the mechanics of standard English are taught in the context of required confessional essays or occasionally in the context of amorphous prejudice masquerading as critical prose. When this class has taught the student that English is incompatible with the language of his daily thoughts and conversations, he is required to take a second course that does for literature what the first did for writing. In this class the student reads an eccentric collection of essays, novels, poems, plays, and short stories compiled by a royalty-hungry editor and presented under various bogus rubrics such as "Theme," "Irony," and "The Omniscient Observer." Here the student learns that literature is moral and meaningful, though useless and boring. Out of the average freshman class exposed to this curriculum, only the die-hard romantics and Kilmeresque creative writers will survive as English majors. The good minds will have fled in disgust.

This curriculum, however, is typical. It has become the pattern for literacy and language training in high schools and grade schools throughout the country and around the world. The result of this method of training will not be clear for several decades, because we have only taught it extensively since the end of the Second World War, when the number of college students with no foundation in the elite texts of earlier generations began to increase. We can, however, make a guess. Students trained in reading and writing and the other technologies of modern civilization but denied exposure to the dominant brand of literacy taught in the select schools will differ in only one respect from their peers who attended vocational schools. They will fill the same functionary positions as the vocationally-trained and be paid similar wages, but, unlike their more resigned peers, they will resent the level of authority and power they have been able to obtain. Their dissatisfaction, whether it turns outward as a political revolt against the society they may feel has cheated them or turns inward as an oppressive sense of failure, is sure to be a powerful force in our culture and in others faced with the same problems of literacy. As members of the job market, these students will feel qualified for social power, and their anguish at not achieving it will be all the more acute because they will not have the critical training in the use of language that would permit them to verbalize and examine their discontent. Having been taught the mechanics of English without the skill for its advantageous manipulation, their cry will be Caliban's:

You taught me language; and my profit on 't
Is, I know how to curse. The red plague rid you
For learning me your language!

The perils of our educational failure are already apparent
in the strategy of the new Republican coalition, which pan-
ders to the frustrated, inarticulate ambitions of the illiterate
lower middle classes. The disaffection of the college-trained
illiterate will find its natural outlet in political power built
on the votes of the ambitious but untrained young. Anyone
who hopes that the younger generations will prove to be a
politically progressive balance to the current conservative
trend should heed W. H. Auden's warning that

In semiliterate countries
demagogues pay
court to teenagers.

ORTHODOX AMERICAN LITERACY

I have several times spoken of the brand of literacy sanctioned as orthodox in American society. What is it? The Educational Testing Service gives as the second reason for the
falling SAT scores an absolute decline among all sorts of students in the ability to use language as examined by the test.
Reporters and educators have been quick to equate this decline with a failure of literacy. But what exactly has failed?

As in any culture, literacy in America is a blend of attitudes toward language with mechanical skill. The Homeric
hero was literate when he could interpret and organize speech
for political ends. In the last century the literate Englishman
employed the skills of reading and writing within a culture
that believed these to be tools for arriving at certain kinds of
worldly truth. In no case is knowledge of the mechanical
means of literacy alone sufficient to make a man literate. He

also has to know the proper uses of language. It was not enough for the seventeenth-century Puritan to read and write. He had also to be able to see a revelation of the divine plan in the scheme of language.

At one time or another Americans have shared all these perceptions of language and have defined literacy accordingly. The Pilgrim fathers preserved Bunyan's sense that language, properly used and understood, reveals a divine message, and the rapid spread of reading and writing skills in colonial New England is due in large part to this perception. Nineteenth-century American oratory was created on the classical model, in which the gaze of the speaker is directed not toward metaphysical speculation but toward the fulfillment of the earthly promise. Lincoln's Gettysburg Address is the culmination of this tradition. In it he looks not beyond the grave but toward the final realization of man's best political ambitions. Americans have also enjoyed a literacy based on the view that language is a means to the discovery of certain pragmatic truths, a notion for which we are heavily indebted to trends in eighteenth- and nineteenth-century English thought. Calvin Coolidge's apothegms illustrate this tendency in American literacy.

Composed of such various attitudes toward language, the literacy of any culture, certainly the American, would seem impossible to characterize in a single formula, but in our own century these different conceptions have at last converged in a single form of literacy that governs communication in America. This form contains all the paradoxes of its multiple origins, yet rests upon certain commonly accepted assumptions about language and its role in life. First among these is that language is not and does not contain a revelation of any superior truth; it is human and flawed. This assertion is by no means obvious or trivial. Its importance is tremendous.

The negative judgment that language contains in itself no

superior truth has European origins. Rousseau denounced language in general as a man-made barrier erected between man's self and his feelings:

> If the study of languages were only a study of words, that is to say, of the letters and sounds that serve as symbols, it would be a suitable study for children. But languages, in changing the symbols, modify also the ideas which those symbols represent. Our ideas are based on our language; our thoughts take a tincture of our idioms. Judgments of fact alone correspond; turns of thought take a particular form in each language.

Language then is only suited for cataloging facts. As soon as feeling is reduced to words, it loses some essential element. The idea has had many godparents, but Rousseau is father of the belief that language, far from being a realization of experience, is a veil over it that we must penetrate in order to reach the primary level of our being. Rousseau's view is now part of American orthodoxy. John Ashbery writes,

This poem is concerned with language on a very plain level.
Look at it talking to you. You look out a window
Or pretend to fidget. You have it but you don't have it.
You miss it, it misses you. You miss each other.

The poem is sad because it wants to be yours, and cannot.
What's a plain level? It is that and other things,
Bringing a system of them into play. Play?
Well, actually, yes, but I consider play to be

A deeper outside thing, a dreamed role-pattern,
As in the division of grace these long August days
Without proof. Open-ended. And before you know it
It gets lost in the stream and chatter of typewriters.

It has been played once more. I think you exist only
To tease me into doing it, on your level, and then you aren't there
Or have adopted a different attitude. And the poem
Has set me softly down beside you. The poem is you.

Ashbery's reflections on the poem are a summary of the American view of language. He says that we have the same relation to language that we have to our selves. We are alienated, unfulfilled. We cannot quite find our selves or each other, and language is the medium of our failure, though we continue to hope it might be the means of our success. Language operates on "a very plain level" that has been made complex by the frustrated expectations we have of it.

Harold Bloom, who presides over a genuinely American school of criticism, makes a similar point in prose: "I myself urge an antithetical criticism in the American grain, affirming the self over language, while granting a priority to figurative language over meaning." The popularity in American academic circles of prolix European writers like Jacques Derrida is a further symptom of the American commitment to a notion of language as obstacle to rather than as vehicle for truth. In this view of language as infinitely obscure, even the most resolute intellectual antagonists may find common ground in our time. Derrida, for instance, has little love for the ideas of his compatriot Claude Lévi-Strauss but both are agreed that language is an imposition, for Lévi-Strauss because within the context of society writing is used for power and aggression, for Derrida because in any context words are a distortion of experience, a reflection of reality always running behind but never coalescing with it. The American experience anticipated the French position. In *East Coker*, T. S. Eliot had already stated the essential antagonism of the modern school toward language:

> So here I am, in the middle way, having had twenty years—
> Twenty years largely wasted, the years of *l'entre deux guerres*
> Trying to learn to use words, and every attempt
> Is a wholly new start, and a different kind of failure
> Because one has only learnt to get the better of words
> For the thing one no longer has to say, or the way in which
> One is no longer disposed to say it. And so each venture

Is a new beginning, a raid on the inarticulate
With shabby equipment always deteriorating
In the general mess of imprecision of feeling,
Undisciplined squads of emotion.

Contemporary science also supports the view of language as obstacle. Gary Zukav's *The Dancing Wu Li Masters*, a book that expounds the elements of modern physics for the lay reader, claims that the mind bogged down in old-fashioned ideas of language and logic can never appreciate the structure of reality because

> *symbols do not follow the same rules as experience.* They follow rules of their own. In short, the problem is not *in* the language, the problem *is* the language.
> The difference between experience and symbol is the difference between mythos and logos. Logos imitates, but can never replace, experience. It is a *substitute* for experience. Logos is the artificial construction of dead symbols which mimics experience on a one-to-one basis. Classical physical theory is an example of a one-to-one correspondence between theory and reality.

The author goes on to dismiss classical physics, and with it the scientific validity of Logos. As his title suggests, the data of modern physics are for him more easily understood by a mind operating with mythos. For Zukav as in Zen, the fundamental nature of reality can only be comprehended by the mind that has transcended language and can contemplate the lively silence that is Being. Logical positivism, the philosophical discipline that has sought to make language as precise a vehicle for scientific thought as possible, finally achieves its goal by dismissing Locke's notion that language conveys truth. For the logical positivist, language is a highly suspect tool to be used only with great caution. Even then, its results are problematical. "If our aim is never to succumb to falsehood, it would be prudent for us to abstain from using language altogether," the positivist A. J. Ayer wrote. Behind his joke lies a restricted view of language that colors our literacy. In our day, the two cultures of science and art have at least agreed to bury Logos.

If, as the modern view holds, language is not only incapable of revealing any superior truth but is in fact an obstacle to our participation in the fundamentals of experience, what uses do remain for it? Rousseau and Ayer both allow that language conveys facts and information about which we may have the greatest practical certainty. The conveyance of facts and information is after all the leading modern conception of literacy's primary but not exclusive function. Ashbery and Bloom and Zukav point us in the necessary direction. For them, language suggests. For Ashbery and Bloom, the figurative language of poetry suggests (but is not identical with) the world of self. For Zukav, verbal symbols suggest a myth that enlightens our mind about the structure of physical reality. In our literacy, literature has become another form of suggestion. It is useful in helping us attain certain physical and mental sensations, but it is not itself these sensations.

American students are brought up on this view of language, and their writing reflects it. Asked to discuss a book or a film, the typical freshman begins his essay "I feel . . . ," as if the whole point of the work had been to conjure up an emotional entertainment for delectation of self. Students resent having to write about literature at all. Verbal reflection destroys the emotional universe suggested by the work. Language may suggest experience, but it can never be experience. Plato or Wycliffe or Bunyan found in language a purified form of experience. The typical freshman essay merely subscribes to the prevailing literacy when it rejects this position.

A further result of the contemporary theory of language is that style becomes at best a means of suggesting certain sensations beyond the grasp of language. At worst, it is a pretense. For Milton or Dr. Johnson style in language did not merely represent or suggest an idea; it became the idea. In our century, however, where language is no longer regarded as having the capacity to embody living ideas, style can no longer serve this function. Within American literacy, style is viewed with suspicion. The dreadful prose styles of even educated writers is a development of this contempt for language. We are used to bad style in most commercial and governmental prose, and now its appearance among teachers of writing confirms that style is no part of our established literacy. "I would like now to go back to aspects of the action-response model of learning other than the quality of the feedback," writes an academic on teaching the art of discourse. Style is dead because the attitude toward language that sustains it has passed away. This is why the English-speaking world cannot at present produce a translation of the Bible or the prayer book to match the seventeenth-century efforts. The sublime sense of language required for this task is gone.

For the same reason rhetoric is a lost art in America except among advertisers. The ideas about the uses of language that shaped Pericles' or Lincoln's oratory have disappeared. Those good speakers we still have now conform to the mechanical literacy at the heart of our culture. Our best public speaking is simple, straightforward, and informative. Attempts at embellishment or elevation in current American rhetoric seem ridiculous because they are not connected with any principle of language alive in either speaker or audience. Like the imitation Tudor and Cape Cod architecture of condominiums, the sham embellishments of modern rhetoric only remind us of what is lost. Advertising, however, generates a truly lively and exciting rhetoric because it is motivated by the living principle of greed and remains in touch with the spoken vitality of the popular language.

Mechanical literacy characterizes our culture as Locke's literacy did eighteenth-century England's. Other notions of language and its uses abound in twentieth-century America, but restricted, mechanical literacy has become part of our dogma. It permeates our educational system, discolors our daily chores, and circumscribes our corporate behavior. It does not represent the only idea about language we have, but it is the one that counts.

The prevailing American form of literacy, while it has a refined intellectual pedigree, makes itself felt in the most mundane details of life. Grade-school and high-school language curricula reflect it. Students reaching college from the American educational system are generally able to write two forms of prose: simple factual statement and straightforward exposition of their feelings. It is extremely unusual to discern in their work anything like a sense of individual style, nor can they easily read or comprehend authors who have such a sense. Their attitude toward language nurtures their uses of reading and writing. Reading and writing as they now occur in America are skills designed for the transference of information and serve the additional function of suggesting certain emotional states that are ultimately beyond the reaches of language. Thus American literacy is neither purely pragmatic nor merely narcissistic, but rather a curious Push-Me-Pull-You, a monster constructed by transplanting the heart of Rousseau into the body of Bentham. It is both fully utilitarian in its practical use of language for transferring basic information and fully romantic in its insistence that language does not embody but only suggests a speechless universe of self-titillation. These seemingly antithetical states of pragmatism and solipsism, far from conflicting, in fact reinforce one another. Both aspects of American literacy deprecate any attempt to assert an inherent truth in language and discourage the notion, vital to centuries of Western thought, that words are an end in themselves, in which we find the fullness of life. Ours is a creed of nominalism broad enough to embrace the systems of Nietzsche and Ayer.

The pragmatic aspect of American literacy is more obvious in our daily lives than the romantic. American educators have for some time debated whether the SAT and other tests designed to measure ability with language ask questions that accurately gauge students' talent and potential. The answer is, "Unfortunately, yes." "Unfortunately" because the kind of literacy that these examinations require is mechanical and devoid of life. "Yes" because those who possess this pragmatic kind of literacy have the best chance of conforming to American expectations for language use.

The SAT treats language as a mechanism for conveying information. By presenting passages for reading comprehension and then demanding that the student find the one correct set of answers, it supports the notion that language either transports information in correct ways or else it fails. A sample test in an SAT-preparation book gives a reading passage about the life of the scholar. "He is one who raises himself from private consideration and breathes and lives on public and illustrious thoughts," opines the passage. The test asks, " 'Public and illustrious thoughts' means: (A) what the people think (B) thoughts in the open (C) thoughts for the good of mankind (D) thoughts transmitted by the people (E) the conclusion of history." All of these answers seem correct to me, but only the student narrow enough—or smart enough to know how narrow the literacy of his society is—will deduce that the testors expect answer (C). The SAT reinforces this narrow view of language in its vocabulary tests, where words have fixed equivalents and opposites. But the sentence completion section of the SAT is saddest and funniest of all:

Though he is an amateur dancer, he has the _____ of a gazelle and the _____ of a professional.
  (A)   awkwardness . . . strength
  (B)   cerebration . . . credulity
  (C)   agility . . . prowess
  (D)   delirium . . . demeanor
  (E)   detriment . . . skill

Answer (E) is not quite English, but the remaining answers seem lively and intelligent, except (C), which is mechanical to the point of being clichéd. A quick mind would pick (A) or (B) or (D). Anyone who wants to succeed within the confines of American literacy, however, had better pick (C).

Narrow as the SAT may be, it is an accurate test of the respondents' indoctrination in the sanctioned literacy of our culture. Success on the SAT therefore is a good indicator of success in college and later life.

Perhaps the most discouraging manifestation of America's bankrupt literacy is the proliferation in our midst of that group of language critics who preach the doctrine of correct usage from their syndicated columns. These champions present themselves as guardians of language and culture. With the cerebration of gazelles and the credulity of professionals they sit in judgment on *hopefully* and *ain't*. That these ubiquitous arbiters of taste have achieved popular acclaim is at once astounding and revealing. I remember watching one of them on an early-morning talk show. He denounced with great vigor the American habit of unconsciously closing routine business with the formula "Have a nice day." I suppose that this phrase is insipid, but I cannot imagine that our civilization needs Jeremiahs because it has fostered among its people a reflex of mutual felicitation.

And yet the public reads their books and columns. I take this adulation to be a misguided form of concern for the preservation of American literacy. But what do these commentators and their audiences believe they are saving? Not language itself, surely, for that goes along with or without public guardians. Instead the critics seek to maintain those grammatical, rhetorical, and orthographic conventions that have characterized white middle-class American English over the last fifty years. Implicit in their labors is a notion much like the one employed by the Educational Testing Service: there exists one form of English usage that may claim to be correct, and all speech and writing should be measured against this model.

In so far as it promotes intelligibility and therefore social and economic prosperity, correct usage as championed by self-appointed guardians of language is the militant expression of the aspect of American literacy that demands mechanical skill in reading and writing for the good discipline and continued productivity of the work force. Common sense and not John Simon is all that is required to inform the ambitious individual in American society that inability to communicate in the linguistic style approved by the leadership of government, industry, and the professions increases the difficulty of joining these ranks or even attacking them in any effective way. To know the correct use of American English is to have mastered the style of language approved by the prevailing middle classes. What is odious in these critics of language is their claim, implied or stated, that correct English represents something more than the chance development of a middle-class language of authority. We are told, more often by their tone than by their words, that those who do not use correct English are uncivilized, unreflecting cretins who offend against culture merely by opening their mouths or applying pen to paper. Thus the pragmatic dimension of American literacy has been sanctified. It has become a tyrannous object of mysterious veneration.

THE NEW LITERACY

The doctrine of correct English in both its practical and quasi-religious aspects has had much to contend with in the last half-century. The natural evolution of language, the introduction and triumph of electronic media, and the democratic process that has increasingly elevated those unskilled in the approved forms of language to positions of popular influence have all worked against it. It survives at all because its benefits for organization outweigh the frustration occasioned by conforming to its restraints. Its continued authority, however, cannot help but give rise to a new, radical literacy, just as occurred in the Roman empire. Then, formal Latin became a written language of imperial power while another literacy, with its roots in the Christian message, grew up beside it and finally absorbed it. We too confront a new, popular brand of literacy, but one that has not yet found a dynamic ideology to give it purpose or direction.

The new popular literacy expresses itself in Americans' almost universal resistance to certain forms of correct English. Correct English, and the mechanical literacy of the middle classes that spawned it, have alienated the writing population just as it was alienated in the Hellenistic age. Today a universal system of mechanical language use according to inflexible rules has helped create two literacies. One is the established literacy taught in schools. The other is a popular literacy keyed to the spoken language of the people. We have one literacy of power and business and another still-forming literacy of popular vigor. This great development reveals itself in small examples. So far as I can judge, for instance, only Americans over forty or those educated in the select few schools that propagate the most exact habits still employ apostrophes with habitual conformity to the established rules. In the population at large, apostrophes to indicate either possession or contraction are an anachronism, and without constant pressure from the educational system, they would have passed out of usage long ago. The *New York Times* now frequently misses the apostrophe in possessives on back pages. Outside New York it disappears on front and back pages. In freshman essays it is nearly extinct. Even threats of corporal punishment could not induce college students to understand the logic or practice the use of the apostrophe. In the evolutionary scheme of the language, the apostrophe is a dodo.

Possessives have always vexed writers of English, and the

apostrophe is an artificial solution to the problem of distinguishing between contractions, genitives, and plurals. The question of apostrophes is only one example among many. Punctuation, spelling, syntax, and grammar are all slowly suffering an evolution in their popular usage that, unhindered by the restraints of correct English, would soon revolutionize the language.

This revolution, were it to succeed, would have been due in part to sloth. It is easier to ignore apostrophes than to trouble with their correct use. Sloth, while always a potent force for simplification in language, is nevertheless not the only force at work in the formation of a new, popular literacy. The same students who resolutely remain in darkness about the niceties of correct English grammar are as capable of intelligence as any previous generation. They are only selective about what niceties they choose to observe. Months of exercises will not shake their nonchalance about commas, but few are likely to misspell the name Led Zeppelin. The new literacy is not a byproduct of cultural delinquency but a felt need among its users. It has evolution on its side, and its claims will be heard.

Heard is the right word, for like its Roman counterpart the new popular literacy is one of the ear more than the eye. The development of electronic media has facilitated its growth, and it finds its readiest means of ideological expression in music. Radio, television, and other sound-carrying electronics systems like tape and record players have been widely blamed for the collapse of literacy. This view is of course highly biased. Literacy from the time of the pharaohs forward has never collapsed but only changed. Those who denounce the new electronic media for corrupting literacy really mean to say that these innovations menace the middle-class literacy approved by the American establishment.

Electronic media are a powerful stimulant to the development of a literacy centered on the spoken word. They threaten established literacy by offering a continuous stream of vernacular raised to the level of popular art—an art without the restraints of correct English. The seemingly disparate programming that fills so much airtime on radio—rock 'n' roll and religious revivalism—has in common an appeal beyond the established mechanical literacy. Both reject the prevailing doctrine that language at best suggests but never itself contains truth. American evangelism's alliance with radio and television could have been predicted from the long fundamentalist Christian tradition that emphasizes the enlightening power of the spoken word. Religious revivalism and rock music both assert the primacy of language and the immediacy of its inherent truth:

> I listened and I heard
> Music in the word,

says Peter Townshend's lyric, "Pure and Easy." Though this particular song evokes Eastern mysticism, it shares common ground with the Protestant ministry of the Christian Broadcasting Corporation. Rock and popular religion are alike fed by the desire of the people at large for a literacy that credits the power of language to capture and express the fullness of life.

Established American literacy, with its emphasis on mechanical skills and its assertion of the limitations of language, thwarts man's desire to feel himself fully represented in words. Evangelism and rock seek to provide the satisfaction of full representation in language, one by the traditional message of the living Word, the other by reviving, in the context of new electronic media, the primal appeal of lyric poetry. Rock demands respect as the first art form of the new literacy. Its lyricism is full of vigor and wit. Like the artistic output of any generation, most of it is trite, but its successes are dazzling. The opponents of rock condemn it by the aesthetic canons of the old literacy which it is the point of rock to reject. Implicit in rock is a new set of standards of beauty and language. The best rock is not just imitation Romantic or contemporary poetry. It is a form that asks to be judged by its own new values. Those who venerate the principles of the old print literacy will likely abominate rock, and indeed rock invites their abomination.

Like earlier popular literacies founded on the apotheosis of speech, it scorns formal language structures for the rapture of the Word:

> Don't know nothin' 'bout no Rise and Fall
> Don't know nothin' 'bout nothin' at all.

The new man, like the first Christians, is proud to be *rudis et indoctus*, uncouth and unlearned. This pride is in part the result of the Romantic aspect of current literacy. Words are suspect and counterfeit. Feeling is spontaneous and genuine. The less I know the more real I am. But the new generations of Americans are not without enthusiasm for language. The pride they take in their ignorance of correct English arises from the passion with which they have devoted themselves to a new type of literacy.

Classes of college freshmen, bored by literature anthologies and wary of traditional poetry, can nevertheless recite whole stanzas of The Who's lyrics from memory and discuss them with zeal. Critics of the new literacy claim that memorization is a lost talent among contemporary students, but in fact their memories are fine. Their ability to retain lyrics, commercials, and other forms of oral expression is capacious. Increasingly, however, they resist memorizing dates and literature associated with the established norms of language. They link this kind of memorization with the mechanical view of language against which their new literacy is engaged. Their supposed failure of memory is highly selective, and their ennui is not a response to all literacy, only to the prevailing literacy. Bruce Springsteen (another difficult spelling few students will ever miss) describes the literate man in rock culture:

> the poets down here
> don't write nothing at all.
> They just stand back and let it all be.

The conjunction of incorrect grammar with immediacy in the apprehension of life is no accident in rock lyricism. It is the essence of the new literacy.

The desire for a vital literacy is not new. As we have seen its roots are in the doctrine of the Logos in the early Church, in the popular aspects of the Protestant Reformation. No matter how refined its pedigree, however, this new literacy is not likely to win friends among the adherents of the old. By its nature it follows the early churchmen in finding the man who is *rudis et indoctus* praiseworthy for this nearness to the truth contained in speech. By its nature, it rejects the structures of formal written English in favor of the enthusiasm of the spoken word. The new literacy, however, is not a polar opposite of the old. The two are already inextricable. Television, that scorned object of smug contempt to the guardians of the existing literacy, does not replace reading and writing so much as alter their practice. The experience of the Renaissance with the introduction of print elucidates the process. Then, print did not dislodge the popular literacy of speech and enthusiasm. Instead it blended with it in ways that modified the destinies both of print and of literacy. A recent study of television viewing among American teenagers indicates that those who at an early age watch the most television programming will at a later age read the greatest number of books. Many of us are familiar with the habit of reading while watching television. The man propped up in front of the tv with an open book in hand is an emblem of the new literacy, which is slowly incorporating the mechanics of the old.

We can hear the process at work in expressions like "record library" or "tape library." Television and film strive for literary polish—their concession to established literacy. Authors constantly use tv or radio to promote their work, and script writers dream of publishing novels. Print meanwhile has become the handmaiden of the electronic media. Screenplays are prolegomena to novels. Even avant-garde writing is often little more than transcribed monologue or dialogue. The best selling magazine in America is *TV Guide*. The papers with mass circulation like the *Star* and the *National Enquirer* retail gossip about electronic-media stars.

The new media will not produce a population of nonreaders or non-writers. They will, though, change fundamentally the way people regard reading and writing, first, by fostering an attitude toward language that believes in the real, inherent power of the Word and, second, by providing new mechanical means for the expression of literacy.

The new literacy, operating through the electronic media, will compel the established literacy of middle-class authority to become looser and more idiomatic. At the same time the established literacy will assert its claim that it alone provides the social and economic cohesion necessary for a productive society. Each brand of literacy will modify the other while purists of each camp watch in horror at the slow contamination of both. If we are lucky, the resulting mongrel product will be a literacy effective enough to serve the needs of social organization and technological development but sensible enough to maintain rapport with the vitality of spoken language and the need of the population for a sublime sense of language. If we are unlucky, the Edwin Newmans and John Simons will prevail. We will have two literacies, one of authority operating through print and known only to an elect handful of scribes trained at elite universities, the other propagated through electronic media and embodying the people's aspirations for an incarnation of the Word in the daily affairs of life. This second result would represent a severing of the body from the soul of our culture. It would pit class against class as well as literacy against literacy. It would be the end of the American experiment.

CHAPTER EIGHT

Conclusion

In a celebrated passage of *The German Ideology* the chief dreamer of the nineteenth century conjures up a picture of the perfect economy, in which the worker hunts or fishes by day and becomes a critic by night, just as he wishes, fitting his humanity to his employment and his employment to his humanity. Behind Marx's utopian vision is a desire for a fully literate world in which every man rejoices in performing the tasks necessary to support life and in the critical mind that permits him to be conscious of his joy. The expansion of consciousness is the first article of the Marxist program, and "language is practical consciousness." This utopia depends on the critical appreciation of language that is the foundation of literacy. In our world, the universal dissemination of reading and writing skills is a realistic goal, but the great majority of people are far from achieving the critical discipline in language that would make Marx's utopian consciousness possible. How could this be accomplished? Is it desirable that it should be accomplished?

The route to achieving literacy is well marked by historical example. Rome, Europe, and America show us that persistent governments can, if they wish, teach their populations the mechanics of literacy. To speak and to hear we learn without formal instruction. The component of literacy that has traditionally required special development is the critical attitude toward language. In most civilizations this attitude has been nurtured in only that segment of the population destined for authority. The process of this nurture has been much the same, whether the culture itself sustained oral or written literacy. Athenian statesmen, Roman senators, Chinese bureaucrats, English aristocrats, American bankers—all have been reared on a diet of language and literature. Their programs of study have often seemed obsessive in their focus on a single subject or language—for the Greeks, Homer; for the Chinese, the Confucian canon; for the churchmen, logic; for the English, Latin; for an earlier generation of Americans, the Bible. The very absorption in such a narrow focus, however, has been the secret of literacy. When studied with singular intensity, the revered text or the syllogism or the dead language requires the mind to think of language in an abstract, interpretive way. Those English aristocrats who had a common grounding in Vergil's *Aeneid* and Horace's odes shared something more than a patina of erudition. They had a common literacy rooted in shared appreciation of the workings of language. The Vergilian quotations that punctuate the Parliamentary debates of the nineteenth century are a clue to the success of the empire. The manipulation of language is a means of controlling the world. Those who are conscious of this manipulation have a powerful tool of authority, and where this tool is shared among a nation's leadership, their behavior will in all likelihood be single-minded and effective. Literacy of this sort is power.

A society that hopes to give its whole citizenry this power must aim to instill critical talent with language. While it is busy teaching reading and writing, the dull mechanical curriculum of modern America ignores the development of this critical talent. Most American students are subjected to a hopelessly divided language curriculum throughout their school life. This curriculum pretends to be humanistic. It encourages discussion of the moral values found in various short stories, essays, and poems while it teaches the basics of grammar and spelling. In fact, this training makes students minimally functional in the mechanics of literacy while it deprives them of the essential language discipline they need in order to make the mechanics of literacy effective. After their exposure to a succession of tawdry literature anthologies from grade school through college, students may be full of beautiful values and charming ideas, but they lack the ability to manipulate these ideas in language, and values or ideas without a means of realization are useless. But students will have been indoctrinated in the mechanical rudiments of established literacy, and while they may despise their studies, they are generally capable of operating at the level of peonage that the system has all along intended for them.

Meanwhile, the dull, pragmatic rationale of established literacy beguiles even the best students into a misguided course of language studies. Language is taught for its practical value, not because it offers the mental discipline for control of the world. Students learn Spanish so they can ask for a hotel room in Guadalajara. The manipulative sense of language, however, is best taught in curricula that have no practical value. The ideal language by which to teach literacy has no mundane utility. The ideal text is a vision in a dead language. Marx, who meant to change the world, prepared himself by reading Aeschylus in Greek once a year. Any society that shares his desire to change the world must commit similar acts of imagination, even against its most utilitarian instincts.

Aeschylus, verbally the most dense and daring of the Greek dramatists, challenges all our standards at once, not least of all our standards of language. That is one reason why Marx delighted in him. The great authors have never written in any standard language. We don't read Shakespeare to learn standard English. We don't even learn standard English to read Shakespeare. If we do, we deceive ourselves. By maintaining that Aeschylus or Milton or Dickens—in short, our cultural tradition—is somehow tied to the preservation of standard English, we implicate the glories of our culture in the alienation that already attends our formal language. Homer and Shakespeare are more likely to be read in the sense that Marx read Aeschylus as soon as we admit that they stand above current brands of authorized literacy. Aeschylus or Shakespeare or the student who reads them each has his own language. Why must they all be reduced to the common banality of correct usage? The liberation of the vernacular would also be the liberation of the classics, as it was in the Renaissance. I am suggesting a world where ordinary students learn Greek and Latin, read Shakespeare in his own words, and still keep their own new literacy. The suggestion is only fantastic because we have become so mired in trivial questions of form and mechanical proficiency that we have forgotten where the strength of our culture lies.

I have already argued that society would give up practical education in formal English only at great cost to social order and economic prosperity. But universal competency in standard English, even if we were to achieve it, would bring us no closer to the kind of literacy implied in Marx's utopian vision. To reach that point we need a curriculum that besides teaching utilitarian skills also demonstrates the connection between language and life.

One way to achieve this end is to allow the nascent literacy of the people to emerge. At present the educational establishment resists the half-formed literacy implicit in rock, in freshman writing, and in the popular evolution of English. Instead we should encourage this new form. We should challenge it to be as conscious as it is vital. The vitality of the new literacy requires discipline and introspection if it is to be a humane force. The longer educational institutions resist the new, the surer we may be of its chaotic hostility.

An astute reader who patiently reviewed these thoughts on literacy objected that I want more than can be had: a vital popular culture and a world where people read Aeschylus. "You can't get to Aeschylus by bypassing standard English," he comments. His remark summarizes the sentiments of concerned citizens throughout the country. They equate the vernacular with barbarism. They imagine that the day the literacy of rock prevailed Aeschylus and our heritage would be lost forever.

I sympathize with this concern but reject its logic. As matters stand, it may be more correct to say that in the future we won't get to Aeschylus by teaching standard English. The Aeschylus whose message is linked to the middle-class norms of language of twentieth-century America is very different from the creator of *Prometheus Bound*.

If it could be accomplished, would it be desirable to fulfill Marx's vision? Everyone must answer this question for himself. We may be sure of two things, however. First, universal literacy of the sort Marx's vision requires would provoke an unprecedented revolution in the world's affairs. It would sweep away the power of specially trained elites everywhere and give to the mass of men a power over their lives that might as easily induce anxiety as elation. Second, the day when Latin, or Swahili, or any curriculum designed to instill critical literacy is taught in the course of an ordinary American education is not within sight.

The reality that we face is the emergence of a new literacy, equipped with the techniques of reading and writing but untrained in the critical uses of language. This new literacy has generated its own attitudes toward language. Its commitment is to the immediacy of the Word, its art form is lyric poetry, its spirit is set against the formal impositions of the old literacy. It only awaits leadership. We can hope that when its leadership comes, it will come from minds like Milton's that can champion the new while preserving the best in the old. There can, however, be no certainty of this. From the perspective of the present, the future of American literacy looks at once appalling and sublime. The age of Alaric also professed a literacy of the Word, full of grace and truth.

Notes

The notes for each chapter give the source of direct quotations in the text. Each reference is keyed to the name of the author or of the work as mentioned in the text.

CHAPTER ONE
Blithering Agamemnon

ARISTOTLE: *Historium animalium* 488a33.

WEST: "The Scandal of Lyric Maugham," letter, *TLS*, May 20, 1980, 499.

CICERO: *Brutus* 81.4, 108.9.

BUSH: "Polluting Our Language," *The Future of Literacy*, ed. Robert Disch (Englewood Cliffs, N.J.: Prentice-Hall, 1973), 65.

KELLER: *The World I Live In* (New York, 1909), 113-21.

BURNS AND ALLEN: in George Burns, *Living It Up* (New York: Putnam, 1976), 57.

JAYNES: *The Origin of Consciousness in the Breakdown of the Bicameral Mind* (Boston: Houghton Mifflin, 1977), 72, 73.

HOMER: *Iliad* 2.1-41, 2.38, 9.31-49, 2.79-83, 19.74, 19.147.

JABÈS: *Le Retour au livre* (Paris: Gallimard, 1965), 22.

CHAPTER TWO
Chief Cobb vs. Themistocles

CHIEF COBB: see *New World Metaphysics*, ed. Giles Gunn (New York: Oxford University Press, 1981), 281-82.

PLATO: *Phaedrus* 275A (the condemnation of writing is actually spoken by Thamus, king of Egypt, in one of Socrates' parables); trans. R. Hackforth, *Plato's Phaedrus* (Cambridge: Cambridge University Press, 1972), 157.

HOMER: *Iliad* 6.168-70 (note that Homer calls the characters written on the tablet "deadly"—a fair summary of how writing was regarded at the dawn of the heroic age).

HERODOTUS: *Histories* 8.21-23.

PLUTARCH: *Lycurgus* 13.1-2 (see also *Moralia* 221B and 237A), trans. Bernadette Perrin, *Plutarch's Lives,* Loeb edition (Cambridge: Harvard University Press, 1914), 1.240-42.

CHAPTER THREE
Word against Empire

POLYBIUS: *Histories* 6.34-35.

ITALIAN ARMY: for these figures, see Carlo M. Cipolla, *Literacy and Development in the West* (Baltimore: Penguin, 1969), 116-18.

MARTIAL: *Epigrams* 11.3.3-4.

EGYPTIAN HYMN: see A. C. Moorhouse, *The Triumph of the Alphabet* (New York: Schuman, 1953), 188.

SUETONIUS: *Octavius* 88.

ALEXANDRIAN GLOSS: see L. D. Reynolds and N. G. Wilson, *Scribes and Scholars,* 2nd ed. (Oxford: Clarendon Press, 1974), 12.

JESUS: John 8.6; Matthew 11.15.

APOSTLES: Acts 4:13.

ORIGEN: *Contra Celsum* 8.47.20-24.

PAPIAS: see Eusebius, *Ecclesiastical History* 3.39.4.

GREGORY OF TOURS: see Erich Auerbach, *Literary Language and Its Public in Late Latin Antiquity and the Middle Ages,* Bollingen series 74 (New York: Pantheon, 1965), 104-5 (Auerbach's trans.).

GREGORY THE GREAT: see H. J. Chaytor, *From Script to Print* (Cambridge: Heffer, 1945), 32.

POPE ZACHERY: see Laurence Sterne, *Tristram Shandy,* ed., James A. Work (New York: Odyssey, 1940), 327, where Work's note gives the story of the barbarian priest.

DANTE: *De vulgari eloquentia* 6.40; trans. A. G. F. Hovell (New York: Greenwood, 1969).

JOHN OF SALISBURY: *Metalogicon* 1.21, 1.24; trans. Daniel McGarry (Berkeley: University of California Press, 1955), 60, 71.

ST. FRANCIS: see E. R. Curtius, *European Literature and the Latin Middle Ages*, Bollingen series 36 (New York: Pantheon, 1953), 311.

CHAPTER FOUR
When Media Collide

MCLUHAN: *Understanding Media: The Extensions of Man*, 2nd ed. (New York: NAL, 1964), 157.

ALFRED THE GREAT: see John William Adamson, *The Illiterate Anglo-Saxon and Other Essays* (Cambridge: Cambridge University Press, 1946), 5.

OLD ENGLISH RIDDLE: in *Anglo-Saxon Poetry*, trans. R. K. Gordon (London: Dent, 1954), 297-98.

AQUINAS: *Summa Theologica* 1.10.

WALTER MAP: *De nugis curialium*, trans. F. Tupper and M. B. Ogle (London, 1924), 8.

M. T. CLANCHY: *From Memory to Written Record: England 1066-1307* (London: Arnold, 1979), 44.

GOETHE: *Faust* 1, 1716, 1718-20.

LOLLARD CONDEMNATION: see Margaret Aston, "Lollardy and Literacy," *History* 62 (1977), 352.

WYCLIFFE: *De officio pastorali*, *English Works*, F. D. Matthew, ed., Early English Text Society 74 (London, 1880), 429; *De veritate* 1.42.

GORDON LEFF: *Heresy in the Later Middle Ages* (New York: Barnes and Noble, 1967), 522.

HARNACK: *History of Dogma*, trans. Neil Buchanan (New York: Dover, 1961), 7, 216.

DONNE: Sermon 23; *Devotions upon Emergent Occasions*, 19, Expostulation.

BUNYAN: *Grace Abounding to the Chief of Sinners*, sections 249, 188.

MORGAN: "Television Viewing and Reading: Does More Equal Better?" *Journal of Communication* 30, no. 1 (1980), 162, 163.

CHAPTER FIVE
Iran to Ann Landers

PALEVI: Inaugural Address, September 8, 1955, *Teheran Congress, Speeches and Messages, UNESCO World Congress of Min-*

isters of Education on the Eradication of Illiteracy (Paris: UNESCO, 1966), 14.

LAINGEN: "Message From Iran," *New York Times,* January 27, 1981, A19.

MALCOLM X: *The Autobiography of Malcolm X* (New York: Ballantine, 1973), 173, 179.

CHAPTER SIX
Hopefully into the Future

LOCKE: *Essay Concerning Understanding,* 3.11, 3.2.

FOUCAULT: *The Order of Things* (New York: Pantheon, 1970), 120 (Foucault's italics).

OWEN: *Revolution in the Mind and Practice of the Human Race: or The Coming Change from Irrationality to Rationality* (London, 1849), 81 (Owen's italics).

MILL: "Considerations on Representative Government," *Collected Works* (Toronto: University of Toronto Press, 1977), 19, 470.

STONE: "Literacy and Education in England, 1640-1900," *Past and Present* 42 (1969), 86.

LENIN: "The New Economic Policy," *Selected Works* (New York: International, 1937), 9, 269-70.

GASKELL: *North and South,* ch. 28.

SIMON: *Paradigms Lost: Reflections on Literacy and Its Decline* (New York: Clarkson Potter, 1980), xvii, 214.

LOCKE: *Essay Concerning Human Understanding,* 3.11.

GASKELL: *Cranford,* ch. 1.

STEINER: *After Babel* (New York: Oxford University Press, 1975), 469-70.

NEWMAN: *Strictly Speaking* (New York: Warner, 1974), 174.

STUDENT PAPERS: From the author's collection of freshman writing (Southampton College freshmen, fall 1979).

CHAPTER SEVEN
Caliban in America

JEFFERSON: *Notes on the State of Virginia, The Writings of Thomas Jefferson,* ed. Paul L. Ford (New York, 1894), 3, 252. For a sample of Jefferson quoted to support modern liberal thinking, see Anthony Brandt, "Literacy in America," *New York Times*, August 25, 1980, A23.

HEW STUDY: *What Students Know and Can Do*, Department of Health, Education and Welfare, 1977 (4518-13), 89-97.

FRESHMAN ESSAY: student paper, Southampton College.

LADY BIRD JOHNSON: item in *New York Times*, November 25, 1980, B6.

SHAKESPEARE'S CALIBAN: *The Tempest* 1.2.365-67.

AUDEN: "Marginalia," *Collected Poems* (New York: Random House, 1976), 593.

ROUSSEAU: *Emile*, Book 2; *Emile*, ed. R. L. Archer (Woodbury, N.Y.: Barron's, 1964), 111.

ASHBERY: "Paradoxes and Oxymorons," *TLS*, October 24, 1980, 1188.

BLOOM: "Viewpoint," *TLS*, May 30, 1980, 611.

ELIOT: "East Coker," *Four Quartets*, 172-82.

ZUKAV: *The Dancing Wu Li Masters* (New York: Morrow, 1979), 276 (Zukav's italics).

SAT SAMPLES: The reading-test sample is taken from *Preparation for College Board Examinations* (Chicago: Regnery, 1972), 172, 174; the sentence-completion sample comes from *How To Take the SAT* (New York: NAL, 1979).

TOWNSHEND: "Pure and Easy," *Who Came First*, MCA, 1972.

SPRINGSTEEN: "Jungleland," *Born to Run*, CBS, 1975.

CHAPTER EIGHT
Conclusion

MARX: *The German Ideology*, in *Selected Writings* (New York: Oxford University Press, 1977), 166, 168.

Bibliography

A very thorough bibliography of works about literacy can be found in Harvey J. Graff, *Literacy in History: An Interdisciplinary Research Bibliography,* with addedum, Newberry Papers in Family and Community History 76-1 and 79-6 (Chicago: Newberry Library, 1976, 1979). The bibliography at the back of *Literacy in Traditional Societies,* ed. Jack Goody (Cambridge: Cambridge University Press, 1968), is also very useful. The following notes do not intend to be exhaustive. I mention those books that seem helpful for a better understanding of the issues raised in each chapter of this book, as well as the most important sources of my information.

CHAPTER ONE
Blithering Agamemnon

The most concise, informed summary of literacy is Jack Goody and Ian Watt, "The Consequences of Literacy," *Literacy in Traditional Societies,* ed. Jack Goody (Cambridge: Cambridge University Press, 1968), 27-68, a lucid overview that invests the attainment of literacy with almost magical force. The essay immediately following it in *Literacy in Traditional Societies,* Kathleen Gough, "The Implications of Literacy in Traditional China and India," 69-83, serves to correct the excesses of Goody and Watt by establishing literacy as a cultural function.

Walter J. Ong has written about literacy in a series of works that give wide scope to the term. *The Presence of the Word* (New Haven: Yale, 1967), *Rhetoric, Romance, and Technology* (Ithaca: Cornell, 1971), and *Interfaces of the Word* (Ithaca: Cornell, 1977) develop the important theme that literacy must be regarded as a part of the larger notion of Word. Ong is both a Jesuit and a child of the sixties, and his work is indelibly stamped by both influences. For him, Word is synonymous with "communicating," and "communications in this sense obviously relates to man's sense of his own presence to himself and to other men and to his sense of God's presence." Stripped of their metaphysical superstructure, these books are full of common sense and insight.

Gilbert Murray defined the literate man in his description of the *grammatike* in *Religio Grammatici* (Boston, 1918). Jacques Barzun, *The House of Intellect* (New York: Harper, 1959), is an elegant attempt to reach an abiding, humanistic definition of literacy. In the last few years there have been a number of attempts to define the term in less classical and more sociological or practical terms: David Harman, "Illiteracy: An Overview," *Harvard Educational Review* 40 (1970), 260-63; Robert L. Hillerich, "Toward an Assessable Definition of Literacy," *The English Journal* 65 (February 1976), 50-55. But the most interesting general speculations of literacy are those of Jacques Derrida, most prominently in *Of Grammatology*, trans. Gayatri C. Spivak (Baltimore: Johns Hopkins, 1976), and *Writing and Difference*, trans. Alan Barr (Chicago: Chicago University Press, 1967). Neither Derrida nor his master Heidegger mentions the term literacy, but much of their work is about it, at least as I have defined the word. The patient reader who can withstand the assault of Derrida's purposely convoluted prose will find that he discusses the question of literacy as it occurs in daily life with rare verve and good sense. Much contemporary criticism in France and America discusses language, consciousness, reading, writing, textuality, authorship, and audience. This criticism is often narrow or overly abstract. A good introduction to the various theories is Robert Young, *Untying the Text: A Post-Structuralist Anthology* (London: Routledge and Kegan Paul, 1981).

Because literacy is intimately connected with notions of language and consciousness, its study ought to be reinforced with readings in the vast fields of linguistics and philosophy. The most challenging short pieces on language that I know are the book reviews by T. P. Waldron, *Modern Language Review* 74 (1979), 117-22, and *Times Literary Supplement,* July 11, 1980, 785. Waldron is always concise and provocative. Celebrated modern texts on language like A. J. Ayer, *The Problem of Knowledge* (New York: Penguin, 1956), Benjamin Lee Whorf, *Language, Thought, and Reality* (Cambridge: MIT, 1956), Edward Sapir, *Culture, Language, and Personality* (Berkeley: University of California Press, 1964), Noam Chomsky, *Language and Mind,* 2nd ed. (New York: Harcourt Brace Jovanovich, 1972), and Geoffrey Sampson's attack on Chomsky, *Liberty and Language* (New York: Oxford University Press, 1979), often indirectly discuss the phenomenon of literacy.

Julian Jaynes's popular book on language and consciousness, *The Origin of Consciousness in the Breakdown of the Bicameral Mind* (Boston: Houghton Mifflin, 1977), is best followed by a corrective dose of real biological study. Michael Gazzaniga and Joseph Le Doux, *The Integrated Mind* (New York: Plenum, 1978), and *Psychology and Biology of Language and Thought,* ed. George A. Miller and Elizabeth Lenneberg (New York: Academic, 1978), present fascinating material holding out the promise that when the biology of consciousness and language are better understood, some of the more puzzling questions about literacy may admit of scientific answers.

Roger Shattuck, *The Forbidden Experiment* (New York: Farrar, Straus, Giroux, 1980), tells the story of the Wild Boy of Aveyron while touching on essential issues about language, consciousness, and literacy in a highly accessible style.

CHAPTER TWO
Chief Cobb vs. Themistocles

The works of Eric A. Havelock and of Jack Goody are the best introduction to the history and uses of reading and writing in the development of civilization. In *Preface to Plato* (Cambridge: Harvard University Press, 1963), Havelock studies how the mechanics of reading and writing are related to the development of ideology and cultural values. This early book is amended by his subsequent work: *Prologue to Greek Literacy* (Cincinnati: Cincinnati University Press, 1971); *Origins of Western Literacy,* monograph series 14, Ontario Institute for Studies in Education (Toronto, 1976); and numerous articles, now collected in *The Literate Revolution in Ancient Greece and Its Cultural Consequences* (Princeton: Princeton University Press, 1982). Havelock sometimes allows his passion for literacy to carry him away. Alphabetization becomes "something like a thunder-clap in human history" because it allegedly spelled the death of oral culture. Despite his naïve belief in the mechanical potency of reading and writing, he establishes with thorough scholarship that "literacy is not a term with a single determinant," that it is social and evolving.

For an anthropological approach to literacy, see Jack Goody, *The Domestication of the Savage Mind* (Cambridge: Cambridge University Press, 1977), where he discusses the characteristics of oral cultures and the influence of reading and writing on "the technology of the intellect." Like Havelock, Goody has a devotion to his subject that occasionally leads him to overstate his case. In *The Domestication of the Savage Mind,* for instance, he theorizes that the introduction of writing leads oral cultures to a more rational, modern, scientific view of medicine. In our own culture, the corpus of Galen's work stifled the growth of medical thought for centuries.

Writing has many historians. J. Gelb, *A Study of Writing* (Chicago: University of Chicago Press, 1952), is still available in paper and is an excellent introduction to the history of alphabets and writing systems. Also useful are B. C. Ullman, *Ancient Writing and Its Influence* (New York, 1932); A. C. Moorhouse, *The Triumph of the Alphabet* (New York: Schuman, 1953); Marcel Cohen, *La Grande invention de l'écriture,* 2 vols. (Paris: Imprimerie Nationale, 1958); and David Diringer, *Writing* (New York: Praeger, 1962).

Plato's *Phaedrus* is the single most important theoretical work on the role of reading and writing in the history of culture. It should be read alongside of the section in the first-century B.C. Greek historian Diodorus Siculus, *History* 12.11-14, on Charondas, reading, writing, and the good life in ancient Thurium. John Oxenham, *Literacy* (London: Routledge and Kegan Paul, 1980), is a brief, workmanlike introduction to the subject. Michael Stubbs, *Language and Literacy* (London: Routledge and Kegan Paul, 1980), is largely about spelling but is somewhat useful.

The books dealing with the biological foundations of literacy mentioned in the bibliography for Chapter One should be supplemented by Jean Piaget and Bartel Inhelder, *The Psychology of the Child* (New York: Basic, 1969); the same authors' *The Growth of Logical Thinking* (New York: Basic, 1958); and L. S. Vygotsky, *Thought and Language* (Cambridge: MIT, 1962).

In addition to Havelock's work on ancient Greece, several other studies of the uses of reading and writing in the history of specific civilizations are also useful in arriving at a better understanding of literacy itself: P. J. Wiseman, "Books in the Ancient Near East and in the Old Testament," *Cambridge History of the Bible*, ed. P. R. Ackroyd and C. F. Evans (Cambridge: Cambridge University Press, 1970), 30-47; Sterling Dow, "Literacy in Minoan and Mycenaean Lands," *Cambridge Ancient History* (Cambridge: Cambridge University Press, 1973), 2, part 1, 582-608; Terrence A. Boring, *Literacy in Ancient Sparta, Mnemosyne* supplement 54 (Leiden: Brill, 1979); F. David Harvey, "Literacy in the Athenian Democracy," *Revue des études grecques* 79 (1966), 585-635, and the same author's "Greeks and Romans Learn To Write," *Communication Arts in the Ancient World*, ed. Eric A. Havelock and Jackson P. Hershbell (New York: Hastings House, 1978), 63-78; C. H. Roberts, "Books in the Graeco-Roman World and in the New Testament," *Cambridge History of the Bible* (Cambridge: Cambridge University Press, 1970), 48-66; L. D. Reynolds and N. G. Wilson, *Scribes and Scholars*, 2nd ed. (Oxford: Clarendon Press, 1974); the sections on the Chinese language and writing system in Joseph Needham, *Science and Civilization in China*, vol. 1 (Cambridge: Cambridge University Press, 1961); Evelyn Rawski, *Education and Popular Literacy in Ch'ing China* (Ann Arbor: University of Michigan Press, 1979).

CHAPTER THREE
Word against Empire

The two best studies of literacy yet written both deal with the relation between notions of language, technologies of expression, and the rise of Christian ideology in the Middle Ages. E. R. Curtius, *European Literature and the Latin Middle Ages*, trans. Willard Trask, Bollingen series 36 (New York: Pantheon, 1953; now published by Princeton), and Erich Auerbach, *Literary Language and Its Public in Late Latin Antiquity and in the Middle*

Ages, trans. Ralph Manheim, Bolligen series 74 (New York: Pantheon, 1965; now published by Princeton), are breathtaking for the compassion that is an integral part of their awesome scholarship.

In *Tristes-Tropiques,* trans. John Weightman and Doreen Weightman (New York: Atheneum, 1974), Claude Lévi-Strauss shows how writing, as well as other forms of "progress," corrupt the beatific existence of primitive, oral peoples. "Conversations with Claude Lévi-Strauss," *The Future of Literacy,* ed. Robert Disch (Englewood Cliffs, N.J.: Prentice-Hall, 1973), 15-19, presents the noted anthropologist's theory in brief compass. Lévi-Strauss on literacy is best read in tandem with Jacques Derrida's zealous demolition of his—and of his master Rousseau's—premises: *Of Grammatology,* trans. Gayatri C. Spivak (Baltimore: Johns Hopkins, 1976), 97-140.

The history of literacy in Rome and through the early Christian centuries is illuminated by Helen Tanzer, *The Common People of Pompeii: A Study of the Graffiti* (Baltimore: Johns Hopkins, 1939); James Westfall Thompson, *The Literacy of the Laity in the Middle Ages* (New York: Burt Franklin, 1963); M. B. Parkes, "The Literacy of the Laity," *The Medieval World,* ed. David Daiches and A. Thorlby (London: Aldus, 1973), 555-77; and V. H. Galbraith, *The Literacy of the Medieval English Kings,* Proceedings of the British Academy 21 (London, 1935).

Mario Pei, *The Story of Latin and the Romance Languages* (New York: Harper and Row, 1976), is a good history of the evolution of formal and popular language in this period. Isidore of Seville, *Etymologiae,* ed. W. M. Lindsay (Oxford: Clarendon Press, 1911), and John of Salisbury, *Metalogicon,* ed. Daniel McGarry (Berkeley: University of California Press, 1955), provide two medieval Christian views of the role of language and language study in the life of culture. They may be read in conjunction with R. H. Robins, *Ancient and Medieval Grammatical Theory in Europe* (1951; Port Washington, N.Y.: Kennikat Press, 1971).

CHAPTER FOUR
When Media Collide

The history of the rise and influence of print receives its definitive treatment in Elizabeth Eisenstein, *The Printing Press as an Agent of Change: Communications and Cultural Transformations in Early-Modern Europe,* 2 vols. (Cambridge: Cambridge University Press, 1979). This book has an extensive bibliography. Marshall McLuhan, *The Gutenberg Galaxy: The Making of Typographical Man* (Toronto: University of Toronto Press, 1962), and *Understanding Media: The Extensions of Man* (New York: McGraw-Hill, 1964), have been attacked by scholars since their appearance; see Jonathan Miller, *Marshall McLuhan,* Modern Masters series (London: Fontana, 1971). Even if McLuhan were totally wrong, his work ought to be read in conjunction with Eisenstein's because of its provocative enthusiasm for grand ideas.

M. T. Clanchy, *From Memory to Written Record: England 1066-1307* (London: Arnold, 1979), establishes the connection between the use of writing and the rise of print. Clanchy meant his book to be a supplement to and an advance on H. J. Chaytor, *From Script to Print* (Cambridge: Heffer, 1945). Chaytor's small book covers vast territory with elegant precision. Franz H. Bauml, "Varieties and Consequences of Medieval Literacy and Illiteracy," *Speculum* 55 (1980), 237-65, is full of jargon but nonetheless contains a stimulating argument that the rise of literacy and written record fundamentally altered European consciousness and literary genres.

For English literacy in the medieval and Renaissance periods, see John William Adamson, *The Illiterate Anglo-Saxon and Other Essays* (Cambridge: Cambridge University Press, 1946); H. S. Bennett, "The Author and His Public in the Fourteenth and Fifteenth Centuries," Essays and Studies by Members of the English Association 23 (1938), 7-24; Francis Wormald and C. E. Wright, *The English Library Before* 1700 (London: Athlone Press, 1958); S. L. Thrupp, *The Merchant Class of Medieval London* (Chicago: University of Chicago Press, 1948); G. A. Malcolm Vale, "Piety, Charity, and Literacy among the Yorkshire Gentry, 1370-1480," Borthwick Papers 50, University of York (York: St. Anthony's Press, 1976). Stephen Greenblatt, "The Word of God in the Age of Mechanical Reproduction," in *Renaissance Self-Fashioning: From More to Shakespeare* (Chicago: University of Chicago Press, 1980), 74-114, elucidates the relation among texts, technology, and creeds in the sixteenth century.

Readers who do not wish to consult Wycliffe's own work can profitably read the sections on him in Gordon Leff, *Heresy in the Later Middle Ages,* 2 vols. (New York: Barnes and Noble, 1967).

Margaret Aston, "Lollardy and Literacy," *History* 62 (1977), 347-71, is an excellent account of the convergence of technology and ideology in the religious convulsions of the fourteenth century.

For other important works on English literacy in the Middle Ages and in the Renaissance, see the bibliography for Chapter Five.

CHAPTER FIVE
Iran to Ann Landers

The best survey of the impact of literacy on development is Carlo M. Cipolla, *Literacy and Development in the West* (Baltimore: Penguin, 1969). Cipolla covers the history of literacy as well as its role in modern economies. Literacy is often assumed to be essential to human advancement and economic prosperity; for this view, see Mary Burnet, *ABC of Literacy* (UNESCO, 1965), and Charles Jeffries, *Illiteracy: A World Problem* (London: Pall Mall, 1967). Recently, more detailed studies have been done to examine in detail the often curious effects of literacy on development. Especially useful is the anthology edited by Léon Bataille, *A Turning Point for Literacy: Adult Education for Development* (New York: Pergamon, 1976). In this collection, the piece by Malcolm S. Adiseshiah, "Functionalities of Literacy," 65-78, is a reasoned statement of the relative role of literacy in culture.

M. J. Bowman and C. A. Anderson, "Concerning the Role of Education in Development," *Old Societies and New States,* ed. Clifford Geertz (New York: Free Press, 1963), 247-79, argues that a literacy rate above 30 percent is necessary for modern economic development. This view is elaborated in C. A. Anderson, "Literacy and Schooling and the Development Threshold," *Education and Economic Development,* ed. C. A. Anderson and M. J. Bowman (Chicago: University of Chicago Press, 1965), 347-67. Albert Meister, *Alphabétisation et développement* (Paris: Anthropos, 1973), contains many interesting speculations about its subject. Prodipto Roy and J. M. Kapoov, *The Retention of Literacy* (Delhi: Macmillan, 1975), argues that literacy is a skill that atrophies with disuse.

A small but impressive body of work argues that literacy is

not a requirement for social or economic advancement. Chief among those holding this view is Harvey L. Graff, *The Literacy Myth: Literacy and Social Structure in the Nineteenth-Century City* (New York: Academic Press, 1979). Graff has edited a useful collection of essays, largely supporting his dissenting view, *Literacy and Social Development in the West: A Reader* (Cambridge: Cambridge University Press, 1982). Shirley Brice Heath, "The Functions and Uses of Literacy," *Journal of Communication* 30, no. 1 (1980), 123-33, supports some revisionist theories about literacy in its findings that the actual uses of literacy are practical rather than aesthetic. E. G. West, "Literacy and the Industrial Revolution," *Economic History Review* 31 (1978), 369-83, surveys a variety of works on literacy and development.

Functional literacy is now a popular concept. An early definition of this term is in William S. Gray, *The Teaching of Reading and Writing*, Monographs on Fundamental Education 10 (UNESCO, 1956). Other basic introductions are *Functional Literacy: Why and How* (UNESCO, 1970) and *Practical Guide to Functional Literacy* (UNESCO, 1973). For some typical questions used in establishing functional illiteracy, see Gordon H. Cole, "The Chains of Functional Illiteracy," *American Federalist* 84 (June 1977), 1-6, and Mark Benedick, Jr. and Mario G. Cantu, "The Literacy of Welfare Clients," *Social Service Review* 52 (March 1978), 56-68. Further afield, Everitt Rogers and William Herzog, "Functional Literacy among Columbian Peasants," *Economic Development and Cultural Change* 14 (1966), 192-202, presents a test case for the value of literacy in developing nations.

The two competing methods of teaching literacy are expounded by their leading advocates: Frank C. Laubach, *Thirty Years with the Silent Billion* (Westwood, N.J.: Revell, 1960) and *Toward World Literacy: The Each One Teach One Way* (Syracuse: Syracuse University Press, 1960), champion the older, more mechanical approach. Paolo Freire, *Pedagogy of the Oppressed* (New York: Herder and Herder, 1970), stresses education as "conscientization."

What statistics there are on world literacy can be found in *The Statistical Yearbook* published by UNESCO. This book relies on the 1980 edition. Also useful are *Estimates and Projections of Illiteracy*, Division of Statistics on Education (UNESCO, 1978); *Guidelines for the Collection of Statistics on Literacy Programs*, Division of Statistics on Education (UNESCO, 1979); and E. A.

Fisher, *Analysis of Literacy Questions in National Census Forms,* Office of Statistics (UNESCO, 1972), which politely theorizes that the Soviet Union fakes its figures on literacy.

The two studies relied upon in this text for information about literacy in developing nations are, for India, H. M. Phillips, *Literacy and Development* (Paris: UNESCO, 1970), and for East Pakistan, Howard Schuman, Alex Inkeles, and David Smith, "Some Social Psychological Effects and Noneffects of Literacy in a New Nation," *Economic Development and Cultural Change* 16 (1967), 1-14. Tom Wick, "The Pursuit of Universal Literacy," *Journal of Communication* 30, no. 1 (1980), 107-12, coins the term superliterates for young American blacks who sport illiteracy as a badge of hostility to white values.

For literacy in Iran, see Pierre Furter, *Possibilities and Limitations of Functional Literacy: The Iranian Experiment* (UNESCO, 1973).

Some psychological effects of literacy are studied in J. C. Carother, "Culture, Psychiatry, and the Written Word," *Psychiatry* 22 (1959), 307-20; Ihsan Al-Issa, "Effects of Literacy and Schizophrenia on Verbal Abstraction in Iraq," *Journal of Social Psychology* 71 (1967), 39-43; and Melanie Klein, "The Role of the School in the Libidinal Development of the Child," *Love, Guilt and Reparation and Other Works, 1921-45* (New York: Delta, 1975). Klein's essay, where we learn that reading and writing are highly sexual activities, is an unwitting satire of Freudian psychology.

Several studies of literacy and development in specific settings have broad implications: Richard F. Tomasson, "The Literacy of the Icelanders," *Scandinavian Studies* 47 (1975), 66-93; Koji Taira, "Education and Literacy in Meiji Japan," *Explorations in Economic History* 8 (1971), 371-94; Gregory Guroff and S. Frederick Starr, "A Note on Urban Literacy in Russia, 1890-1914," *Jahrbücher für Geschichte Osteuropas* 19 (1971), 520-31; and Le Thanh Khoi, "Literacy Training and Revolution: The Vietnamese Experience," *A Turning Point for Literacy,* ed. Léon Bataille (New York: Pergamon 1976), 123-36. Sylvia Scribner and Michael Cole, *The Psychology of Literacy* (Cambridge: Harvard University Press, 1981), a study of the uses of writing among the Vai people of West Africa, confirms by detailed anthropological and psychological study the conclusion that literacy does not automatically guarantee any mental gain and that literacy differs in kind and effect from culture to culture.

CHAPTER SIX
Hopefully into the Future

There are two excellent studies of British literacy from the Renaissance to the beginning of the industrial era: Lawrence Stone, "Literacy and Education in England, 1640-1900," *Past and Present* 42 (1969), 69-103, and Thomas Laqueur, "The Cultural Origins of Popular Literacy in England, 1550-1850," *Oxford Review of Education* 2 (1976), 255-75. David Cressy, *Literacy and the Social Orders, Reading and Writing in Tudor and Stuart England* (Cambridge: Cambridge University Press, 1980), is the product of a long career of data collection and confirms that literacy was largely a function of class. But see Patrick Collingson's review of Cressy, *TLS*, January 9, 1981, 31.

For literacy in Britain after the industrial revolution, see R. K. Webb, *The British Working-Class Reader, 1790-1848: Literacy and Social Tension* (London: Allen and Unwin, 1955), and R. S. Schofield, "Dimensions of Illiteracy, 1750-1850," *Explorations of Economic History* 10 (1973), 437-54. For Schofield, literacy is a consequence, not a cause of industrialization. The gloomy assessment that literacy is not much help to the working classes finds varying degrees of support in Roger Smith, "Education, Society, and Literacy: Nottinghamshire in the Mid-Nineteenth Century," *University of Birmingham Historical Journal* 12 (1969), 42-56; Michael Sanderson, "Literacy and Social Mobility in the Industrial Revolution in England," *Past and Present* 56 (1972), 75-104—but see the reply by Thomas Laqueur, "Literacy and Social Mobility in the Industrial Revolution in England," *Past and Present* 64 (1974), 96-107; G. H. Bancock, *The Implications of Literacy* (Leicester: University of Leicester Press, 1966), and Claud Cockburn, "A Scepter'd Insularity," *New York Times*, November 18, 1979, E19.

Richard Hoggart, *The Uses of Literacy* (Boston: Beacon, 1961), is a study of the reading done by the English working classes and its influence on English civilization. It should be read in conjunction with two other fine books, H. S. Bennett, *English Books and Readers, 1475-1557* (Cambridge: Cambridge University Press, 1952), and R. D. Altick, *The English Common Reader* (Chicago: University of Chicago Press, 1963). Taken together, the three books give a panoramic view of English reading habits since Caxton.

Michel Foucault, *The Order of Things* (New York: Pantheon, 1970), brings to the study of the uses of language in the European eighteenth century the intellectual excitement of Curtius and Auerbach without matching their scholarship. More detailed studies of language theory in the eighteenth century include George H. McKnight, *Modern English in the Making* (New York, 1928), and Sterling Andrus Leonard, *The Doctrine of Correctness in English Usage, 1700-1800,* University of Wisconsin Studies in Language and Literature 125 (1924). No one should leave the subject of correctness in usage without consulting Noah Webster, *Dissertations on the English Language,* 1789.

The three leading popular guardians of English in America are Edwin Newman, *Strictly Speaking* (New York: Bobbs-Merrill, 1974), William Safire, *On Language* (New York: Times Books, 1980), and John Simon, *Paradigms Lost: Reflections on Literacy and Its Decline* (New York: Clarkson Potter, 1980).

CHAPTER SEVEN
Caliban in America

Literacy in pre-revolutionary America is covered in Kenneth A. Lockridge, *Literacy in Colonial New England* (New York: Norton, 1974), and two books by Richard Beale Davis, *Intellectual Life of Jefferson's Virginia* (Chapel Hill: University of North Carolina Press, 1964) and *A Colonial Southern Bookshelf* (Athens: University of Georgia Press, 1979). De Tocqueville's *Democracy in America* is still indispensable for an understanding of how literacy works within the American system. For literacy in America from colonial times to the modern period, see Charles Warren, *Illiteracy in the United States in 1870 and 1880* (Washington, D.C., 1884), Sanford Winston, *Illiteracy in the United States* (Chapel Hill, 1930), and Lee Soltow and Edward Stevens, *The Rise of Literacy and the Common School in the United States: A Socioeconomic Analysis to 1870* (Chicago: University of Chicago Press, 1981).

The single best survey of literacy and education, complete with statistics, is *Education of the American Population,* a 1960 Census Bureau monograph (Washington, D.C., 1967). Other useful census and demographic materials include *Illiteracy in the United States: November 1969,* Current Population Reports, Population

Characteristics, Bureau of the Census (P-20, 217), March 10, 1971; *What Students Know and Can Do*, Department of Health, Education and Welfare (4518-13), 1977; *The Digest of Education Statistics*, 1980, National Center for Education Statistics, Washington, 1980.

There is a prodigious literature bemoaning the condition of American literacy, laying the blame in various quarters, and announcing solutions. Carmen St. John Hunter and David Harman, *Adult Illiteracy in the United States: A Report for the Ford Foundation* (New York: McGraw Hill, 1979), gives a very thorough picture of the mechanical problem. Mina P. Shaughnessy, *Errors and Expectations* (New York: Oxford University Press, 1977), is the standard text for teachers, describing the rationale and techniques of remedial language education. Stephen Judy, *The ABCs of Literacy* (New York: Oxford University Press, 1979), contains an extensive bibliography on current curricular approaches to literacy. Jonathan Kozol, *Breaking the Bonds of Adult Illiteracy in the United States* (New York: Continuum, 1979), proposes some radical solutions to our dilemma.

For a sample of the concern bordering on hysteria generated by the topic of literacy, see Nat Hentoff, "The Greatest Consumer Fraud of All," *Social Policy*, November/December 1977, 83-86; Paul Cooperman, *The Literacy Hoax* (New York: Morrow, 1978); Thomas G. Wheeler, *The Great American Writing Block* (New York: Viking, 1979); "The Decline of Literacy Is No Illusion," editorial, *New York Times*, March 22, 1980, 20; J. H. Cameron, "The Idea of a Liberal Education," *Commonweal*, April 11, 1980, 201-7; Anthony Brandt, "Literacy in America," *New York Times*, August 25, 1980, A23; and Carol Hymowitz, "Remedial Bosses: Employers Take Over Where Schools Failed To Teach the Basics," *Wall Street Journal*, January 22, 1981, 1, 22.

Donald Holden, "Why Professors Can't Write," *New York Times*, February 4, 1979, E19, explains that educators have no style. Gene Lyons, "The Higher Illiteracy," *Harper's*, September, 1976, 33-40, blames the illiteracy of the professoriate on their pomposity.

Reading, its teaching, and its relation to worldly success are studied in Duane M. Nielsen and Howard F. Hjelm, *Reading and Career Education* (Newark, Delaware: International Reading Association, 1975); David Yarington, *The Great American Reading Machine* (New York: Hayden, 1978); John P. Robinson, "The

Changing Reading Habits of the American Public," *Journal of Communication* 30, no. 1 (1980), 141-52; and George F. McEvoy and Cynthia S. Vincent, "Who Reads and Why," *Journal of Communication* 30, no. 1 (1980), 134-40. David G. Winter, David C. McClelland, and Abigail J. Stewart, *A New Case for the Liberal Arts* (San Francisco: Jossey-Bass, 1981), makes the case that liberal-arts training in colleges correlates highly with success in the marketplace.

The impact of new media on traditional literacy is discussed by Neil Postman, "The Politics of Reading," *Harvard Educational Review* 40 (1970), 244-52; Michael Morgan, "Television Viewing and Reading: Does More Equal Better?" *Journal of Communication* 30, no. 1 (1980), 159-65; and Diana Zuckerman, Dorothy Singer, and Jerome Singer, "Television Viewing, Children's Reading and Related Classroom Behavior," *Journal of Communication* 30, no. 1 (1980), 166-74.

To my mind the best diagnostician of the larger social and linguistic problems behind the current literacy crisis is George Steiner, *In Bluebeard's Castle: Some Notes Towards the Redefinition of Culture* (New Haven: Yale University Press, 1971) and "After the Book," an essay that appears in an excellent anthology, *The Future of Literacy,* ed. Robert Disch (Englewood Cliffs, N.J.: Prentice-Hall, 1973), 145-57. Also good in this collection are Herbert Marcuse, "The Closing of the Universe of Discourse," 73-87, on the relation of correct usage and social structure; Louis Kampf, "The Humanities and Inhumanities," 117-26, on the sham culture of American business; and Paul Goodman, "Format and 'Communications,'" 89-99, on the link between linguistic and spiritual bankruptcy in the young. The anthology, *The State of the Language,* ed. Leonard Michaels and Christopher Ricks (Berkeley: University of California Press, 1979), is also full of stimulating pieces and may profitably be read with Roger Scruton's review of it, *TLS,* February 22, 1980, 211-12.

Two short pieces on the definition and direction of literacy in the modern world are of importance. Johan Galtung, *Literacy, Education and Schooling—For What?* University of Oslo papers 56 (Oslo, 1977), makes the distinction between mechanical proficiency and critical ability. Andrew Schonfield, "Can Literature Compete? A Radio Discussion between Andrew Schonfield, George Steiner, and Julian Mitchell," *Listener,* July 25, 1974, 121-22, presents two widely divergent views in brief.

The diagnosis that a moody brand of narcissism lies at the heart of our culture's troubles was most forcefully made by Irving Babbitt, *Rousseau and Romanticism* (1919; New York: AMS Press, 1976). Babbitt's theory is reincarnated in Christopher Lasch, *The Culture of Narcissism* (New York: Norton, 1978).

For information about the Educational Testing Service and the Scholastic Aptitude Test, see William Angoff, ed., *The College Board Testing Program* (New York: College Entrance Examination Board, 1971); *On Further Examination: Report of the Advisory Panel on the Scholastic Aptitude Test Score Decline* (New York: College Entrance Examination Board, 1977); and Allan Nairn et al., *Class in the Guise of Merit: The Reign of the ETS* (Washington: Ralph Nader, 1980).

CHAPTER EIGHT
Conclusion

Several years ago on a talk show Norman Mailer advised college students to take Latin, Greek, and other apparently useless subjects not learned on the streets. My conclusion is indebted to his remarks. Two articles in *Basic Writing* 3 (Fall/Winter 1980) are stimulating: E. D. Hirsch, Jr., "Culture and Literacy," 27-47, and Orlando Patterson, "Language and Ethnicity and Change," 62-73.

Index